# CALM THE F*CK DOWN

## The Only Parenting Technique You'll Ever Need

BY DAVID VIENNA

VENICE, CALIFORNIA

Published by Knock Knock
1635-B Electric Ave.
Venice, CA 90291
knockknockstuff.com
Knock Knock is a registered trademark of Knock Knock LLC

Conceived and written by David Vienna
www.TheDaddyComplex.com

Illustrated by Erica Salcedo Saiz

This book is a work of humor meant solely for entertainment purposes. It is not
intended to recommend or advise regarding how to raise children. The publisher
and anyone associated with the production of this book do not advocate child
abuse, neglect, or breaking the law. In no event will Knock Knock be liable
to any reader for any damages, including direct, indirect, incidental, special,
consequential, or punitive damages, arising out of or in connection with the use
of the information contained in this book. So there.

ISBN: 978-160106664-0
UPC: 825703-50040-0

10 9

Dedicated to the four people who taught me the most about love and kindness: Larissa, Wyatt, Boone, and Mister Rogers—all of whom can rock a cardigan.

# TABLE OF CONTENTS

## DEVELOPMENT

## BEHAVIOR

## PARENTING STYLES & SKILLS

## PARENTHOOD

## REAL PROBLEMS

# INTRODUCTION

## INTRODUCTION

I'm not a parenting expert ... Wait. Let me back up.

Hi, I'm David. Nice to meet you. That jacket looks nice. It brings out your eyes.

I'm the father of five-year-old twin boys, Wyatt and Boone. Well, they're five years old as of this writing. By the time the book comes out, I assume they'll have aged a bit. Our house looks like a monster truck drove through it more days than not, we almost never have time to cook a real meal, and sometimes I lose my cool around my kids. And by "sometimes" I mean "almost daily and twice on Sundays." So I'm about as far from a parenting expert as you could get without hopping on a rocket and heading to the Andromeda galaxy.

But a lot of parenting experts don't seem to know what they're talking about anyway, with the obvious exceptions of parenting guru Dr. Spock, who encouraged parents to trust their instincts, and *Star Trek*'s Mr. Spock who said, "Without facts, the decision cannot be made logically. You must rely on your human intuition."

And don't get me started on parenting experts who don't have kids. Seriously, that's like getting a job as the host of a cooking show when you've never eaten bean dip out of a can while standing over the kitchen sink. You need to experience the lows to strive for the highs.

Frustration with the deluge of parenting advice led me to write a post on my parenting blog, The Daddy Complex, called the CTFD Method. CTFD stands for Calm The F*ck Down. The technique calls on parents to stop worrying about whether or not they are the best mom or dad in the world and just be a parent. It's based on the belief that a less stressful home environment benefits kids, that common sense can see you through pretty much any parenting scenario, and that we're all screwing up all the time—and that's OK.

I'm not too savvy on internet analytics terminology, but I believe the technical term for how well the post did is: cray-cray with a side of bananas. People all over the world discussed it online, on TV, on radio, and in print. They applied it to things outside of parenting, like writing and wedding planning. And there's even a mental health clinic that now offers classes in how to apply the CTFD Method. I told you: cray-cray with a side of bananas.

The CTFD Method resonated with people in a way I never expected. I wanted to explore it further as a nonexpert struggling through the everyday challenges of parenting. Y'know, like a real person. And because I'm not a complete idiot, I enlisted the help of two actual professionals to make sure I didn't leave the facts behind in the pursuit of a good penis joke. Cyndi Sarnoff-Ross is a licensed psychotherapist with almost twenty years of experience in the fields of clinical psychology and organizational management. Heather Harrison is Assistant Director of Evidence Based Practices at UCLA's National Center for Child Traumatic Stress. And in case you're wondering, they're both mothers.

So, in these pages, you'll find practical applications of the CTFD Method for the first few years with your child—covering behavior, nutrition, development, and, um, biology—and a smattering of facts to illustrate why CTFD works in each scenario. Hopefully, this will help you understand why all parents need to stop putting unnecessary pressure on themselves and calm the f*ck down. But if you disagree, stay stressed, I guess. Like I said, I'm no expert. I haven't even figured out how to shower on a regular schedule.

If the introduction hasn't enticed you to read *Calm The F\*ck Down* by this point, I suppose there's nothing else I can do. I mean, I'm not going to do something as shameless as flirt with you. That would be unprofessional.

Anyway, that's it. I hope you dig the book. And I wasn't kidding about that jacket. It really does bring out your eyes.

# NEWBORNS
# & INFANTS

# MY BABY WON'T POOP

You've mastered the quick butt cleanup. No loaded diaper or runny turd fazes you. Like a skilled gunslinger, you just set your steely gaze against the blinding fumes, grit your teeth, and execute the task with precision and flair as shopkeepers and townsfolk stand and cheer. When it comes to wiping your baby's rump, you are Wyatt freaking Earp.

Except your baby's tushy seems to have shuttered the shop. Though her appetite remains healthy, no poop of any shape, size, or consistency has deigned to show itself for an entire day. As sheriff of this sleepy one-butt town, you think things are quiet . . . a little *too* quiet. Because if she's not evacuating her bowels, that means she's surely filling up. The output she used to dump into her diaper—which you silently hated—you now miss, like an old fecal friend. If left alone, this backup could do the kind of biological damage usually reserved for train derailments and St. Patrick's Day pub crawls.

And you know this isn't right because she usually craps multiple times per day. Even you poop once a day—twice if you visit the all-you-can-eat buffet. You're thinking it's time to bring out the special weapon. Your trusty tool to dispatch any blockage is a massive howitzer that goes by the name "enema."

## CTFD

Your baby will poop, not pop. Breastfed babies can go for up to seven days without pooping and still not have a medical issue, so chances are nothing's wrong. Just keep the diapers on and check her for signs that she might be straining to push something out. (If so, this might signal constipation.) Be patient and when she does finally let go, prepare yourself for a cleanup that will test your faith in biology, humanity, even gravity. To be safe, if your baby hasn't pooped in four or five days, call your pediatrician. Worst-case scenario, the doctor will probably tell you to try a suppository to get those bowels moving. And I'll go ahead and prescribe whatever you need to erase the resulting poop from your memory.

## MY BABY'S POOP SHOOTS OUT

You've heard the horror stories about changing diapers. But you once had a dog with a twitchy stomach, so you feel you're prepared to handle a diaper blowout or two. To get ahead of any possible fecal chaos, you change your baby's diaper at the first sign of discomfort, hoping to avoid an overwhelming mess.

Then it happens.

During a changing, a jet of greenish muck shoots out. And it keeps coming. And coming. And coming. It won't stop.

Now your changing table and part of the wall bear a scatological Jackson Pollock painting and you feebly try to comprehend how that much fluid came out of your son. And what's with the color? That shade of green wouldn't look at home in a nature preserve, let alone dripping onto the bright tones of the rug in your nursery.

There's no way this is normal. It can only mean one thing. Your boy somehow contracted a rare disease that liquefies baby innards and mentally cripples parents.

──────────── **CTFD** ────────────

Congratulations! You've just earned a parenting merit badge. Sew it to your sash and wear it proudly because everyone who's ever changed a diaper has experienced the poo fountain. A newborn's fecal matter, which ranges in colors from "Dockers slacks" to "Pride Parade," is nearly always fluid. That's because your baby's biology changes a lot in the first few months. For their first bowel movements, they literally evacuate cells and other stuff they got while inside the birth mother. Later, everything from what's in the breast milk to what type of formula you might supplement with affects the poops' consistency, color, frequency, and . . . um . . . trajectory. And, yes, sometimes there's a soul-crippling amount of it. Other parents feel your pain, but you're on your own for the cleanup.

## MY BABY WON'T BREASTFEED

When it comes to feeding your daughter, doctors and nutritionists all agree that, until scientists perfect a futuristic food pill, nothing beats breast milk. It provides everything a growing baby needs, including white blood cells to help build up the immune system. Then why doesn't your girl want the boob?

You've researched techniques, gone to lactation experts, and taken classes. But your baby shows as much interest in breastfeeding as she does in electrical quantity surveying. Trying to get your little one to latch on proves an aggravating exercise in futility, and on the rare occasion you do get her to do it, she quickly pops off. You relay stories of your breastfeeding sessions like a sport fisherman who nearly landed a sizable trout: "I almost had her."

Plus, you're missing out on something that's unquantifiable: emotional attachment. Those same experts who tout the benefits of breast milk also claim it aids in creating a special bond between mother and baby, one that guarantees your child will call every weekend and send a bouquet each Mother's Day. Conversely, babies that don't get breast milk and don't form that emotional bond grow to become socially crippled half-wits or, worse, politicians.

### CTFD

Yes, breast milk is rad and all, but the most important thing is that your baby gets fed. So, after your baby's sucking muscles develop, if it turns out she simply prefers the bottle, just pump or use formula and feed her that way. Keep trying to get her to latch on, but know that holding your baby while feeding her a bottle will provide all the nutrients and emotional bonding needed. Besides, your pediatrician will let you know if your girl needs more sustenance and may suggest supplementing breast milk feedings with formula feedings to help with her development and weight gain. We did that for one of our sons who, as an infant, thought "rail thin" was a perfectly acceptable body type.

# MY BABY HAS A MISSHAPEN HEAD

When it comes to sleep positions, back is best. That's what they say. You might not know who "they" are, but they have PhDs and other impressive accreditations. So just trust them. And while we're at it, don't feel threatened by the fact that I have a Doctorate in Divinity from the Universal Life Church. You, too, can achieve the same goal with determination, an internet connection, forty dollars, and a bottle of Central Coast Pinot Noir. But I digress.

Because sleeping on his back is known to help prevent Sudden Infant Death Syndrome (SIDS), you make sure your baby lies supine each night, face toward the ceiling, perhaps even checking in on him during those rare stretches of actual sleep to make sure he hasn't rolled over onto his side. You even try those little foam blocks meant to keep him from spinning, but find them to function less as a restraint and more like an aid to help him roll onto his side.

Thanks to your vigilance, he has never slept on anything other than his back. And now his head looks like a skillet.

All that sleep spent in the same position has caused his soft head to smush like a wad of Play-Doh. You have created the world's only two-dimensional baby. He will have a distinct aerodynamic disadvantage in track and field events. But his haircuts will go faster.

## —————— CTFD ——————

This condition, "plagiocephaly," is common. As he grows, most likely his head will round out on its own. Make sure he gets lots of non-back time when awake. If his head doesn't seem to fix itself by six months of age, your doctor may recommend "helmet therapy," which involves futuristic headgear to aid in reshaping the head. If that occurs, you are allowed to tell people your baby is a space traveler.

Also, once he's out of the danger zone for SIDS (around twelve months of age, or sooner if your pediatrician says so), you can start adjusting his sleep positions to help balance out his head. Though that's long after they start rolling over on their own, so adjusting him may prove futile. Oh, and those foam blocks? Doctors don't recommend them anyway. And before you ask, experts unanimously advise against using duct tape.

## MY BABY ATE SOMETHING OFF THE FLOOR

You're in the kitchen slicing zucchini, proud that you've organized your life enough to actually cook a real dinner for once. Your baby coos as she explores the linoleum tiles. This image of a happy home and a happy baby grew in you from the moment you first talked about expanding your family. You turn to share a glance with your child to capture the feeling like a mental movie. She won't remember it when she's older, but you know it will somehow affect her positively as she grows.

And when you turn, you see her shovel a clump of dog hair into her mouth.

If you have your wits about you (which you won't), you drop the knife before you run to her, scoop her up, and jam your fingers in her mouth to scrape out the tuft of Rex's gray fur. Worse, Rex's fur is white. The clump of hair turned gray thanks to all the dirt and crumbs and, yes, dust mites hiding in corners and crannies. Oh, that mental movie just got a lot more like a Japanese horror film.

As your baby cries and you scrape her tongue with your fingers, you cycle through all of the terrible illnesses she could possibly get from ingesting dirty canine hair: cold, flu, sore throat, heartworm, *E. coli*, rabies. And you wonder who might judge you if you completely shave your dog.

**CTFD**

Not only is dog hair not toxic, it's edible. But only in the way cardboard is also edible. Of course, that's just in the biological sense. You shouldn't actually serve up Australian Shepherd Fur Casserole at a party. Monitor your baby for signs of illness such as nausea or fever, but most likely she'll be more traumatized by your reaction than her hairy appetizer. Not only that, exposure to dirt, fur, and other stuff could actually help reduce the risk of allergies and asthma. So your baby might as well get that stuff from ol' Rex.

On a related note, one of my earliest memories involves me shouldering our Old English Sheepdog out of the way to eat her food from her bowl. Aside from a predilection for chasing tennis balls and barking at the mailman, I turned out fine.

# I'M FREAKING EXHAUSTED

While you were expecting your first child, everybody joked, "Get all the sleep you can now," as if you could build up a sleep bank. You knew it would be a challenge, that you'd be tired, but you were ready. Plus, you had a wild succession of all-nighters in college. You've since learned no amount of sleep pre-baby could have helped you once he arrived. After four months of no substantive rest, you want to track down everyone who made that joke and stomp on their foot. But even if you could track them down, you're too tired to stomp.

You only get sleep in two- to three-hour blocks because your baby needs to be fed eight to twelve times a day. And those blocks only happen if you fall asleep right away, and don't lie awake thinking about all the work and chores to do—scheduling a babysitter, paying the bills, prepping dinner, laughing maniacally at the wall for ten straight minutes. "Sleep when the baby sleeps" is one of those things that only apply in theoretical situations, much like time travel and saving some of your dinner to take home. And that's not the worst part.

This type of sleep deprivation actually makes you go bonkers. Yes, you clinically go mad. More than once. Sometimes for weeks at a stretch. There's a reason they used it at Gitmo as a torture technique. During these times, you can feel your sanity snap like a dry twig, and rational thought becomes a cloudy memory. You do and say and think terrible things that, upon reflection, chill you to your soul—like maniacally tweezing your eyebrows or touting the joys of klezmer disco music—making you question if you ever had the qualities of a decent human being at all.

In time, you'll get what could be considered a normal amount of sleep. (The first time that happens, you will feel euphoria akin to eating a plate full of marijuana brownies while riding a unicorn.) You will also start to see things like your baby's smile or a look of recognition on his face as you enter the room. That, sir, is pretty freaking cool, and it starts the milestone marathon, which includes rolling over, solid foods, crawling, first words, standing, walking, hugs, drawing, and maybe a garage band.

And as for parents of "dream babies"—rug rats who sleep through the night from day one and have no trouble napping—when you meet these people, you can go ahead and stomp on their feet. It's like a freebie the universe provides for sleep-deprived parents.

## NO ONE UNDERSTANDS HOW STRESSED I AM

Your husband's great aunt comes by to see the new baby. During her visit, you mention how long it's been since you've had a real vacation. She waves her hand, dismissing your complaint by saying, "Oh, you're home all day with this darling girl. Every day is a vacation." At that moment, you come close to punching a nice old lady in the throat.

You'd like to ask her if being a batty, geriatric fart is similarly relaxing but think better of it. She doesn't realize that she's just played a key role in your stress. Aside from diminished faculties thanks to sleep deprivation, you find the tensions and mental breakdowns hard to explain and can't accurately convey the feelings to others. Because of that, people think it's not a big deal.

This, of course, adds further frustration, leading you to spend the first three months of your daughter's life muttering to yourself as you hug your knees and rock back and forth in the corner of your bathroom.

 **CTFD**

"1950s Housewife Syndrome," a term I just made up (hmm, I'd better trademark that), encapsulates all the panic, stress, and gloominess that naturally come with the role of stay-at-home parent, and that are too complicated to explain to someone not going through them. As a stay-at-home parent, you must have coping mechanisms or stress relievers in place—like yoga or demolition derby driving—to deal with 1950s Housewife Syndrome™. If you don't, figure some out fast. Even something as simple as getting out of the house once a day can help your mood and sanity.

And though you should certainly keep trying to voice your emotions, don't expect anyone but other stay-at-home parents to understand how you deal with it or why you'd even need to. No, not even your spouse or partner. It will only lead to more stress. Look for parenting or other peer groups if you can. And seeking professional help does not have anything to do with your abilities as a parent. Just remember, when it comes to learning to cope with the inherent stress in your day, there are no wrong answers. Well, except punching old ladies in the throat. That's a wrong answer.

## MY BABY WON'T SLEEP THROUGH THE NIGHT

Despite your repeated efforts to calm your baby boy, he starts crying at midnight and doesn't wear himself out and fall asleep again until 2:30 AM. That marks the beginning of a solid two minutes of blissful sleep, which ends with another fussy session that lasts until 4 AM. He then falls asleep again for a whopping eleven minutes (a new milestone!), just enough time for you to start to doze before attending to him again. Every night plays out this way. Wake, calm the baby, doze, wake, calm the baby, doze. Lather. Rinse. Repeat.

You've tried various sleep training methods, from the Cry-It-Out to the No-Cry Solution, and every variation in between, all of which have left *you* in tears. You've tried playing lullabies, white noise, rain forest sounds. In a weak moment, you've even resorted to smooth jazz. You've discussed it with your parents and asked them what sleep training technique they used on you. They replied with a confused look and asked, "What's sleep training?"

One morning, while washing bottles in the sink, you look out the kitchen window. The sun has yet to show itself. You hear your son start to cry again. Just for a moment of peace, you consider leaning forward and running full speed into the fridge to knock yourself unconscious.

 **CTFD**

If there were a solution to getting a baby to sleep regularly, the inventor could retire on his or her own private island—something modest, like Australia. There are no easy answers to this one. But if it makes you feel better, everyone goes through it. So, there's that.

If you have a spouse or partner, take turns. If your partner puts up any form of protest, make him/her take a turn anyway and fight about it later. If the whole thing gets to be too much, take a break in whatever way you can. Don't hesitate to ask for help from a neighbor, in-law, delivery person, passing stranger, or a stray dog. And your son will sleep through the night soon ... or eventually ... at some point, sleep will happen. Rest assured.

## WE'RE GOING ON A PLANE TRIP

Even with a well-behaved kid (read: "dosed with Diazepam"), the current airline experience would make any parent run for the nearest Zen meditation center (read: "bottle of Diazepam"). Yet you're faced with a flight to see the in-laws for the holidays. Just thinking about the list of items you must get through airport security makes you want to chuck everything and raise your baby in a yurt.

If her diaper is full, it might count as a container. Is pee on the TSA's list of approved liquids? And will her stroller even fit through the security gate? Will it cause a bottleneck at the screening area?

Plus, you remember those flights before you had a kid. When a baby or toddler started freaking out six miles above the Earth, those parents became the most hated people on the plane, even more hated than the guy expelling garlicky belches and hassling the flight attendants.

You briefly consider letting your little girl roam the aisle while onboard to stretch her limbs and keep her from flipping out while trapped in the flight cabin. Then you quickly dismiss the idea after remembering that the floor of the modern airliner is like the movie theater floor's slutty cousin.

And what about nap time? That can't be mimicked on a flight. At home, you take your daughter to her room and dim the lights. On a plane, babies go from sitting to continuing to sit. Just stating "It's nap time" doesn't quite do it. You're pretty sure threats don't work either.

You consider canceling the visit until either your in-laws make the trip themselves or scientists perfect teleportation technology. Even then, though, you're concerned the stroller won't fit through the transporter door.

Here's how it works: you have to send everything except the baby through the X-ray machine. You're usually allowed to take full-sized containers of baby food, hand sanitizer, diaper cream, etc. through. Yes, ignoring TSA regulations (like a common terrorist) is just one of the many perks of parenthood. If you have a stroller, some airports will allow you to get in the shorter Family or Wheelchair lines for screening.

If you've heard the anecdotal tip of dosing your baby with Benadryl to make her sleep thoughout the flight, a word of caution: on some babies, it has the exact opposite effect, essentially giving you a spastic chipmunk to manage for the duration of the trip.

Either way, if you can arrange to sit near other parents, do it. They won't be bothered by any shenanigans like other passengers. Once on the plane, to tackle the ear pressure thing, do a bottle on the way up and a bottle on the way down (or a lollipop if she's older). Bring a duffel bag full of toys your baby has either never seen or hasn't seen in a while. If all else fails, give her a copy of *SkyMall* and she'll occupy herself by tearing the thing to ribbons. Your baby may nap, but most likely you'll have to put on the longest show of your parenthood, with no intermission and no applause.

On the bright side, if any of the flight attendants are parents, you may get a free Bloody Mary.

# TODDLERS

# MY TODDLER WON'T STAND UP

Your wee one doesn't care to stand. He's content to just sit and play with his little plastic frog. And when he needs to get somewhere, he crawls from one room to the other, showing no curiosity about how the hall may look from a standing position. Sure, your guy will stand if you pin him against the coffee table. But when not physically propped up, he just goes back to sitting. And holding his toy frog above his head like a treat for a dog results less in standing and more in crying jags.

Your friend's toddler can stand and even take a few wobbly steps, the showoff. So what's your kid's problem?

All the literature and internet discussions indicate he demonstrates a developmental lag or, worse, extreme laziness. If he shows no interest in learning to walk now, perhaps he'll never learn. That means you'll have to find one of those baby walker things in preschooler size, then kid size, then adult size. Or maybe you could just tie him to a skateboard and tow him around like a pet.

He won't make the football team because he'll never crawl fast enough. You're already factoring in the expense of kneepads that match his wedding tuxedo so he may proudly clomp down the aisle on all fours.

---------------- **CTFD** ----------------

Our son Wyatt didn't even try to stand or pull himself up, while his twin brother Boone spent most of his waking hours trying to master balance and walking. Then, the day Boone made it down the hall walking on his own, little Wyatt looked at us, stood up, and *ran* down the hall to meet his brother. He hasn't stopped running since. I mean, seriously, the kid has no first gear.

Your son will stand when he's ready—whether tomorrow, in a couple of months, or longer. Pretty much all toddlers toddle at some point. And if some sort of physical impediment kept him from hoisting himself up, you'd most likely have noticed it by now. He'll get curious about it soon enough, and once he's plodding around the place and knocking collectibles off shelves, you'll long for the day he wasn't quite so mobile.

# MY TODDLER BUMPED HER HEAD

You were prepared. You lined every corner with foam or soft rubber. You eradicated every sharp angle and hard surface in your home, effectively creating a somewhat inviting padded cell. The living room, the kitchen—the whole kitchen—the whole place, really, looks like your decorator convinced you the next big trend in interior design was sponge.

So you watch excitedly as your little girl pulls herself up, holding onto the coffee table to steady herself. Her eyes widen as she takes in the living room from a whole new vantage point. As drool dribbles from her mouth, you know the thought blaring in her mind: "I can see my house from here!"

Then, weeks or months later, come the first few cautious steps. Like a tipsy frat boy, your girl methodically and clumsily puts one foot forward, then the other. She ventures slowly past the comfort of the soft rug onto the hardwood floor. And when you squeal with parental joy, your little girl stumbles and thumps her head on the floor. As you rush to scoop her up, you curse yourself for not encasing her in layers of bubble wrap.

Checking her head, your worst fears are realized— the beginnings of a bruise. This sort of brain injury could lead to problems down the road, like an inability to learn the letter Q or an affinity for twenty-four-hour news networks.

---------------------- **CTFD** ----------------------

Every toddler gets bumps and bruises. That's why they're called "toddlers" and not "walkers." Even if the bruise becomes a raised bump, it's usually OK. If the area seems concave or if there's a deep laceration, however, seek immediate medical attention. Otherwise, just clean the wound or apply a cold compress like you would for anyone else who bonked their head. And work on your gasp reflex because you'll witness many more such tumbles before she masters the art of the saunter. Also, don't get too freaked out about covering every hard angle with padding. Your toddler will naturally gravitate toward whatever you didn't cover. It just happens. They're like danger magnets.

## MY TODDLER FEARS OTHER PEOPLE

As a parent, you love your child more than you even thought you could, which makes your need for some occasional space a tad confusing. But you've made peace with that dichotomy, and instead try to focus on the serenity of those few moments when the grandparents or friends visit and you can hand him over to them. Endless games of peekaboo may make you feel like you're stuck in one of Dante's lesser known circles of Hell, but visitors find it nearly as enthralling as your son does. You're happy to let them do it and other toddler games for a half-hour while you down a glass of wine or twelve.

Except your toddler physically and vocally refuses to be held by anyone else. Even your coworker, who speaks fluent toddler thanks to her brood of younger cousins, can't entice your son into her arms. No, your toddler sees a face other than yours and hides behind your legs, clutches your shirt or, perhaps, wraps his legs around you so tightly he could win a Brazilian jiu-jitsu tournament.

Your boy wants to permanently attach himself to you like a conjoined twin. (And we've all seen enough Discovery Channel documentaries to know that conjoined twins have a very difficult time at parties and other social functions. Just think of the tailoring bills.) You insist everything will be fine, but he disagrees. He whines, cries, and ramps into a full-tilt meltdown, and your grip on reality loosens, leaving you to serenely float away into the vastness of insanity.

--------------------------------- **CTFD** ---------------------------------

This clinginess phase happens to almost all kids. When it's stressing you out, try to imagine your life about a decade further on, when your son will roll his eyes at the thought of sharing a home with you, let alone the couch. You'll beg for that clinginess. That said, at the toddler stage, it's important to encourage him to let others hold and play with him. Try sitting with the other person and letting him or her interact with your kid. Repeat this until he seems OK for a handoff. Then head to the kitchen and get to that wine.

## MY TODDLER FIGHTS NAP TIME

She's not a daughter, she's a squall with arms and legs. She leaves dirt and destruction in her wake as she moves, plays, dances, screams, tries to climb the armoire. This inexhaustible storm of a child has no limit, as evidenced by her complete disinterest in napping. You, on the other hand, could nap at any possible time, including during a colonoscopy.

During nap time on a good day, she rolls around and fidgets for an hour before you give up. On a bad day, she cries as though tortured or performs an escape from her room that rivals the Anglin brothers' and Frank Morris's escape from Alcatraz.

Each time you put her down for a nap, you watch the baby monitor, hoping the moments of stillness and silence become a long stretch signifying sweet relief. Alas, those patches of quiet always end in a thump or a coo, letting you know your daughter will soon make an appearance in the kitchen, as if she's done with this game called "napping."

To add to the frustration, she actually seems to get more energy around nap time. When all other children of the world lie sleeping soundly midday, your daughter grows manic, emotional, and spastic. She's like your college friend who thought the best way to prepare for the next day's exam was to pull an all-nighter, preferably drunk.

Perhaps your daughter doesn't need a nap. Perhaps this is her superpower. Yes, you've given birth to the next stage of human evolution, one that doesn't require sleep and is enthralled with Oscar the Grouch.

**CTFD**

Kids can start dropping naps at around two years old. And even as they approach that date, your child's world gets more interesting every day. Naturally, she won't want to miss a thing. But just as you'll teach her to say her first words or feed herself, you have to help her learn to nap. If she cries, go to her, but don't pick her up. Just put a hand on her chest and assure her you're in the next room. Then leave again. If she jailbreaks, put her back without any fanfare. She'll eventually learn that time of day she must stay in bed, and sleep will soon follow. Also, if you dose her with NyQuil*, she'll wake up in a week.

*Not recommended by any sane person.

## WE'RE ALWAYS LATE

Ever since your baby transitioned into a toddler, you can't seem to arrive on time for anything. Ever. Your friends simply assume that when you say you'll be somewhere at 10 AM on Monday, it means 10:30 AM. And that's if things go well. If not, it means Thursday. To compensate, you've learned how to commute to work at speeds that would make a top fuel dragster look like a Fisher-Price tricycle.

You battle through the morning routine, the bedtime routine, mealtimes, and any other activity that has a specific start time. Even if your son is in a helpful mood, the steps inevitably take much longer than planned because of any combination of the choices below:

- Refusing to eat

- Wanting to be fed by you

- Arguing for why *Dora the Explorer* should be watched right now

- Running and/or screaming

- Unhappiness with the choice of clothes, even if said child picked them out

- More running and/or screaming

- Hunting for a specific toy that was absently flung across the room the previous night

- Conversation about whether or not giraffes dance

- Even more running and/or screaming

──────────── **CTFD** ────────────

I know what you're thinking, but adjusting the timeline to start the process earlier doesn't help. It just gives your child more time to mess around. Toddlers simply have too much to do to adhere to your randomly chosen schedule. Just getting in the car takes ten minutes, unless of course you've allotted ten minutes for it, in which case it will take twenty minutes.

Though it's absolutely infuriating, there's a fantastically simple solution: Make peace with being late. Go to bed each night knowing the next morning will feature you barking instructions and requests at your son over and over, followed by a mad dash to (hopefully) make it to work on time. Because of that adjustment, you'll sleep better and enjoy your mornings more. Sometimes, you may even prolong that conversation about dancing giraffes.

## MY TODDLER THROWS IRRATIONAL FITS

When your son was a baby, he cried for many reasons—hunger, tiredness, a fall, realizing that pure journalism died long ago—but you could always address them. Now that he's a toddler and actually toddling, however, you discover that you apparently commit a terrible offense multiple times per day, and he has no problem expressing his very verbose disappointment in you.

Once he first started figuring out how to walk, all he wanted to do was stand, cruise, take first steps, and then race against Usain Bolt. Now, when you try to put him on the changing mat, you witness such insanity, you think he's doing a Gary Busey impersonation.

The kicker is it happens pretty much every diaper change. No matter how jovial his mood milliseconds prior to laying him down, you know you must prepare for your own little a cappella death-metal show.

And the changing table is just one of a laundry list of triggers. Your boy doesn't care how exhausted you are. He only seems to care about how loud and long he can shriek for the most inane reason.

To combat this, you implement a technique based on the logic that, for now, you're bigger and stronger than a toddler. You hold him down on the changing pad until the spasms stop. Either that or you distract him with something extremely absurd, like stories by Shel Silverstein or transcripts from a Senate hearing. You also wonder if your friends might frown upon you for bragging that you bested your child in a test of strength or for adding industrial restraints to a changing table.

Blast through that diaper change (or whatever your task is) while he's freaking out. He may get louder and more physical, so dodge those thrashing arms. Then, experts suggest you let your kid wind down before you do anything. He won't hear a thing while in meltdown mode. Once he's calm, you can try asking your toddler what upset him, specifically using words like "frustrated." An even more effective tactic is simply responding favorably when he is accommodating. It teaches him there are better ways to deal with frustration than an emotional Chernobyl. That's much better than my original solution, which involved forcing my boys to repeatedly watch the "Blue Is Frustrated" episode of *Blue's Clues* and telling them to "stop being such a pill."

# MY TODDLER BITES OTHER KIDS

Your wonderful little girl has started biting. More than that, you actually caught her leaning in, mouth agape, trying to get her friend's hand in her mouth to take a bite. She's like a wee little zombie.

Every parent of toddlers you've met talks about fights at playdates or at daycare that make *WWE Raw* look like a sorority house pillow fight. And you're OK with that, but you want her to fight clean. For you, biting during a fight is cheating . . . unless you're losing. Then all bets are off and she should bite wherever and whomever she can.

All right, so your daughter might not have the timing and grace of Muhammad Ali at this age (she barely has the timing and grace of a 1985 Yugo), but you can't teach her to fight fair because then it will seem to her that you're simply encouraging her to fight. Plus, you can't ground a twenty-month-old. If you tried, she'd probably just bite you.

As you let your mind wander, musing about how to handle her cannibalistic tendency, she takes the opportunity to sink her teeth into her friend's arm. Panic explodes in the playroom. Children and parents scatter. On the way home, you swing by the pet store to see if there's a muzzle that might fit her or a chew toy shaped like her friend.

--- **CTFD** ---

When your toddler bites, you should tell her what she did was wrong and why, but don't make too big of a show of it because if she associates it with attention—whether negative or positive—she may do it again, much the same way I repeatedly tell people how I once got my mom's car up on two wheels just because two of my high school friends thought it was a cool story. Show how her actions made the other child feel, ask her if she'd like that to happen to her and how she can make the other kid feel better. This helps build empathy. If these tactics don't work, you're supposed to remove the child from the situation and then do the stern talking thing. If you have to, leave the playdate (or the park or wherever you are). It may be embarrassing for you, but it'll show your child the gravitas of the situation. Actually biting your child in retaliation is, of course, off limits, despite the fact that she probably tastes great.

# MY TODDLER HAS A FEVER

Since he entered daycare, your little boy's nose won't stop running. You've phoned your relatives and told them to buy stock in the Kleenex company, because thanks to you, sales are booming. One day, however, your son appears lethargic and you take his temperature. The thermometer reads in the triple digits. And while you'd love to see hundreds in your wallet, seeing one on the thermometer doesn't prove as joyous.

Those ads from your childhood about leaving your pet in a car during summer flash through your mind. "Hot enough to fry an egg?" the ad said, "hot enough to fry a dog's brain." You panic, trying to guess how hot the pan must be to fry an egg. You just assume it's 100 degrees.

Then the vomiting starts. Though you spent the majority of your college graduation night hunched over a toilet, you hoped to spare your son the same experience. And worse, he's not even drunk. Germs have no sense of justice. If they did, they'd leave your boy and find a new host, someone more deserving of this illness, like the Stedmans down the block. They totally deserve to be sick. Have you seen their gaudy holiday lawn decorations?

 **CTFD**

When your child has a fever, call your pediatrician and she'll tell you to come in if it reaches a certain temperature. She might also advise you on ways to cool the kid down. Yes, a high temperature sucks for your child, but in most cases it's not dangerous until it gets *really* high. Opinions vary from doctor to doctor on what that number is. Ask your pediatrician for specific guidelines. If your child is vomiting, it could be a number of things—food poisoning, stomach bug, cold—each of which will pass. Your doctor can check just to rule out something else. (A recent head injury coupled with vomiting, for example, can be dangerous.) And for the record, it takes a temperature of about 150 degrees to fry an egg, and for your kid to get that hot he'd have to be ablaze.

# PRESCHOOLERS

# I CAN'T TRUST A BABYSITTER

Pre-baby, your New Year's Eve tradition usually involved sitting around the house drinking wine and complaining that you weren't invited to any parties. Post-baby, you sit around the house, drink wine, and complain that you wouldn't have been able to attend the parties to which you weren't invited.

Never mind that the last time you actually did attend a party you had to feign interest while listening to a guest with gaudy sunglasses, which may or may not have been ironic, tell you about his brilliant historical-fiction screenplay that pits author Herman Melville against a crime boss called "The Whale." Now you feel like you can't leave the house, and that makes the idea of attending any type of social function all the more enticing, annoying conversations be damned.

The walls of your bedroom bear the chiseled scars and lines that mark your days in this prison. And the tiny warden has, once again, assigned you the demoralizing task of cleaning up her potty accident.

You long for just a single night of freedom, but you have to be at home to care for your girl, because nobody could ever care for her as well as you could. This is your fate—shackled to your offspring until she heads to college.

 **CTFD**

I hate to break it to you parents, but that's just not the case. I mean, it's a child, not a nuclear device. You can get stuck in a rut thinking you *can't* go out and do something. And anyway, at some point, you're going to have to leave your kid in the care of another person. So you might as well try it now. Start small. Let a babysitter or family member watch your child for a few hours while you run errands. Eventually, you'll feel fine leaving the kid for a night so you can go out to a nice dinner, drink wine, and complain that you weren't invited to any parties.

Oh, and if your kid goes to college and it's anywhere near you, you'll still see her every few weeks when she has to do laundry. So, y'know, keep that in mind.

# MY PRESCHOOLER WON'T TRY NEW FOODS

Nutritionists suggest modeling your diet using a food pyramid that includes vegetables, fruit, meat, grains, and dairy. You offer these to your child in various forms, presenting plates arranged with homemade entrées and sides that would even impress your mother, who thought you only knew how to cook a peanut butter and jelly sandwich.

Yet your preschooler has designed his own food pyramid consisting of just mac and cheese. He won't allow anything to pass his lips that didn't come with a bag of cheddar powder. You argue that he needs to branch out, that a diet of nothing but starches works if he plans to compete in a triathlon, but playing freeze tag in the schoolyard doesn't count. Somehow, you manage to wear him down to the point where he agrees to at least take a bite of something new. And you eagerly watch as he raises an asparagus spear to his mouth, takes the most minuscule bite, and then proclaims he hates it.

This charade plays out for every new food item, so you decide to involve him in the cooking process by asking him what he would like. He suggests a cheeseburger and you squeal with glee—not because it's healthy, but because it's something new. With fresh ground beef and perfectly melted cheese, you create the most magnificent slider to ever grace a child's plate. You place it in front of him, he takes a bite, and makes the standard melodramatic yucky face.

You cave. Weeping, you polish off an entire platter of sliders as you make him a bowl of mac and cheese. At the market, you fill your shopping cart with box upon box of his favorite dish. As the clerk rings you up, he casts a cautious glance your way and quietly shudders at the depth of your culinary despair.

Have you ever eaten the same thing for lunch more than a few days in a row? By the final day, your body and mind kinda scream for something new. Well, just as your body tells you what it needs, your kid's body will crave varied fare eventually. He's just a little more . . . focused right now. (And to be fair, mac and cheese is pretty amazing. I mean it's not only mac, but also cheese.)

Continue to offer new dishes and, if you dare, allow him to pick the menu from a list of healthy options, and where he'll eat it. Though nutritionists frown upon bribery, you can also make his favorite dish contingent on him eating a portion of something else. Contrary to what these professionals imply, your child will not turn into a compulsive gambler or a divorce lawyer if you bargain now and again. But keep the dishes simple, like a chicken breast. Save the Oysters Rockefeller for a later date.

## MY PRESCHOOLER WON'T LISTEN

When your child reached toddlerhood, she smiled at the sound of your voice. Eager to make you happy, she joyously helped you with simple tasks and obeyed the house rules. But now that she's a preschooler, she's acting in a manner so rude and destructive, you'd kick her out if you weren't afraid she'd wreak havoc on the city like a chicken-nugget-obsessed Gamera.

She shakes the little bottle of blue paint as you tell her not to shake it. She even looks you in the eye as she does it, covering your kitchen table with cobalt streaks. She asks for a cookie though you've already said no three times. Now she only smiles at the sound of your voice when you let her get her way. Her thoughts about the house rules? Screw 'em. And your happiness only interests her when it suits her needs. Seriously, who does she think she is? Congress?

You ponder the possibility that a child as young as your daughter could produce enough ear wax to effectively block out the specific tone of your voice. Your pediatrician said the hearing tests went fine, but he must have done it incorrectly. A hearing problem certainly exists, because there's no way your adorable daughter would willingly disregard the things you say.

Because if she won't listen to you now, she won't listen to any other authority figures either—teachers, managers, coffee shop baristas. She'll never learn to play by the rules—especially the Rule of Law. Signs warning "Shoplifters Will Be Prosecuted" will *inspire* her to steal. After a handful of arrests, she'll end up in the stockade and join a prison gang to survive her sentence. When she finally gets out, she'll hug you with arms covered in jailhouse tattoos and request that you call her Spider.

All kids go through this sort of mini-rebellion. Only a small percentage of them end up in prison. The two main reasons your daughter seems not to listen are: 1. She's deeply into what she's doing while you're talking and 2. She's testing how far she can push you. Now, that last one doesn't make her a complete jerk (just a partial one). That's how she learns nuanced personal interaction. She learns by doing, so she needs to understand how much of what you or others say truly matters. To remedy it, ask her to repeat back what you've just told her and issue appropriate consequences, or simply pick your battles.

And remember, you're not in a foreign country. Speaking louder won't help.

# MY PRESCHOOLER HITS OTHER KIDS

All parents look for signs that foretell what their kids will be when they grow up. Your kid loves building with Lego bricks, so he'll be an architect. Your kid enjoys drawing, so he'll be an artist. Using this criterion, you're positive your preschooler will be an Ultimate Fighting Champion because he kicks, pushes, and scratches other kids. You once even saw him deliver a perfect Muay Thai elbow strike to the new kid in his preschool class.

You've explained why hitting is wrong; you've explained that it's not nice to hurt others. You've even tried a diverse and comprehensive collection of punishments. Yet your son's legacy continues to be the series of minor injuries delivered to classmates and peers. Every kid's birthday party you attend degenerates into a series of stern talks with him about playing nice and not hurting others. Every visit to the play-ground ends with an awkward apology to a stranger about your son's behavior. You consider the possibility of not attending future birth-day parties, perhaps homeschooling not by choice but by necessity, or moving into a remote mountain cave where your feral child can freely body-slam unsuspecting deer and woodchucks.

Somehow, the worst has happened. Your kid is the bully.

You're going to find out what it's like to be the villain's mom as your boy punches and shoves his way through life. "He was such a sweet boy," you'll say to the evening news reporter in the wake of some awful thing he does as a teen. You're not sure what that awful thing is yet, but you guess it will involve a busload of nuns and a cliff.

At this age, this behavior usually is not the result of dealing with anger. (That comes later in the book.) Pushing, scratching, and hitting at this stage are usually the result of frustration caused by lack of language. After all, no kid comes out of the womb or even day care with a usable lexicon. Kids get frustrated that they can't communicate and act out physically. You've heard parents repeating "Use your words" ad nauseum? This is why.

Basically, you just need to work with your kid on his vocabulary. Start simple—words like "happy" and "sad," not "trepidation" or "ennui." Help your child find words and say them while stressing that hurting others is wrong, but don't offer both lessons at the same time. It'll take years for your kid to master multitasking. Or, as in my own case, even after growing up, it'll remain as elusive a skill as ninja fighting. Eventually, he'll build a library of words large enough to effectively communicate and the acting out should go away. In the meantime, carry around a few pieces of candy to bribe the kids your son hurts into not telling their parents.

## WE'RE CONSTANTLY SICK

Along with welcoming a new life into your house, you also welcomed a horde of germs. It's like your daughter came with a contagious entourage. And now that your girl's started preschool, she picks up colds pretty frequently. Actually, the word "frequently" doesn't accurately convey exactly how often your child brings home an illness. "Daily" would be more precise. And it's not just colds. Oh, Lord, no.

Your daughter seems to maintain a runny nose pretty much from age two to age four. Not off and on, but a two-year-long runny nose. The only variables are how much it runs and the color of the snot.

And whatever bug she picks up you get as well. She touches everything, she wants to share your food—your home could make a great location for a Hazmat team training class. Plus, the illnesses are like nothing you've experienced. Somehow, the colds and stomach bugs toddlers pick up hit adults exponentially harder. When your child gets a cold, she will maybe have a restless night and a cough. When you get it, it will be an apocalyptic-style plague that will leave you whimpering for help through clogged sinuses and a ravaged throat.

Your kitchen, where you used to prepare delicious meals and snacks, now holds nothing but a massive stockpile of teas, juices, soups, and bottles of vitamin C pills. You've forgotten what healthy feels like. Officials will certainly quarantine your home, leaving you boxed in with the source of your illnesses. You want to cry and scream, but it would just hurt your throat. And you don't have the energy, anyway.

Of all the illnesses my boys have brought home, I only managed to avoid getting one. And that's because I locked myself in the bedroom with a week's supply of SpaghettiOs and the complete DVD collection of Sergio Leone films.

At this age, every place where children gather functions as a petri dish of germs. Your child will have a series of colds and other bugs that are perfectly nonfatal. But believe it or not, this series of bugs helps your daughter's body build up immunity. You should wash your hands often, but by the time you see your child sneeze, it's already too late. Washing your hands at that point is just to teach her how to do it. She'll eventually grow out of getting sick every other week. In the meantime, however, you might also show her how to work the can opener so she can feed you SpaghettiOs when you're too weak to feed yourself.

## MY PRESCHOOLER EXHIBITS DANGEROUS BEHAVIOR

You're watering your garden in the backyard, wondering if the tomatoes you planted will ever come in. Behind you, your son rolls his toy truck up and down the back patio. You don't notice when the sound of the wheels stops or when you hear him drag the truck down the few steps as he makes his way to the playset in the middle of the yard. Why would you? You're planning a bruschetta recipe.

Only when you hear his cry do you turn to see him straddling the truck at the top of the slide. And he's not whining because he's scared. He's whining because he needs you to dislodge his stuck foot so he can continue with his attempt to take the plastic vehicle down the ramp on a one-way trip to Awesomeville.

Though you have limited knowledge of the film industry, you're certain no production would hire a three-year-old stuntman. This attempt at a daring feat follows last week's displays of bravery, which included leaping from the armchair to the coffee table, climbing the bookshelf, and riding the dog down the hall like a Shetland pony.

The bruises, the scrapes, and the minor injuries he gets in these pursuits—none of it dissuades him from trying more and more risky exploits. You fear the dangerous acts will only escalate as your child grows, until he finally does himself in while attempting to ramp his Big Wheel over a row of buses at Caesar's Palace.

Actually, the dangerous acts will continue, and there's a chance he will get more than a bump or a cut. By now, he's probably seen that Superman can fly and the Hulk can lift a car. At this age, he's figuring out his limits, what he's capable of, and where the neighborhood alleys are should he need to change into his vigilante costume. So let him do the stuff that's not really dangerous. If he wants to jump from the picnic bench to the grass, let him. If he wants to sprint down the hall and dive onto the couch, that's OK. To him, these acts are just as exciting and educational as rocketing down the slide on his truck. Of course, supervise him and perhaps even help him out by giving some useful advice (e.g., "Bend at the knees when you land," or "If you're going to roll down the hill in a trashcan, try the plastic one."). And know that those scrapes will happen, and they're necessary. They help him learn that if he wants to leap a tall building in a single bound, he'll need a lot of safety gear. And probably an awesome theme song.

# MY PRESCHOOLER IS FASCINATED WITH GUNS

You want your son to understand that guns are dangerous. Sure, you played army as a kid, charging the battlefield of your neighbor's yard while trying to pick off as many of your best friend's battalion as possible. But those were simpler times, when mustaches were unironic and televisions were thicker than a Buick Century sedan.

So you've asked your father to put his Remington in storage and you prescreen all cartoons searching for gunplay. Each time you pass a police officer and see a holstered sidearm, you explain to your son how and why guns are used. You stress the mantra "guns are not toys," and you go so far as to refrain from allowing any toy guns in the house. When you point at something, you make sure your thumb remains down, lest he think you're advocating "finger guns," a clear gateway to real ones.

Yet despite all this caution, your son finds a way. You first notice it while he draws a picture of a car. He holds his maroon Crayola out and says, "Pew! Pew!" Then, at the park, he and his friends all hunt for sticks bent at a right angle. Then, like a wee General Patton, your son stands atop the slide, waves his arm toward an invisible platoon, and calls to his troops, "Shoot them!" They charge across the playground aiming their sticks and firing imaginary bullets, turning the enemy into a crimson mess so horrific, you're glad they're imaginary.

 **CTFD**

Depending on a few factors, the DNA of a child may feature a few things you might not expect. Namely, a fondness for princess dresses, trucks, dolls, and, yes, guns. Even if your kid never sees a Disney film and knows nothing of hereditary monarchies, she (or he) most likely will want to don a frilly pink gown and a shiny tiara. Guns are no different. Plus, your kid will pick up cues from places over which you have no control—friends at school, glimpses of movie posters. Just keep the dialogue about gun safety going. And those moments between battles as he must defend the playground make a great opportunity to touch on that topic. You can also try encouraging peaceful diplomacy with the enemy, or at least an interest in cross-country skiing for that biathlon.

# MY PRESCHOOLER RUINS EVERYTHING

Childproofing protects your kids, but you can't seem to protect your home (or anything else) from your kids. Nothing escapes damage—the drapes, the bathroom faucet, your psyche, not even your new minivan.

You love that van. It makes it easy to haul around your daughter, a dog, and whatever other crap you need. That new-car smell affects you like a fine perfume or a plate of fettuccine Alfredo. But while driving north for a holiday weekend, your little girl projectile vomits a sippy cup's worth of milk all over the interior. In fact, she somehow evacuates more milk than she took in.

So just three months after buying it, you shell out a sizeable chunk of change to have the thing detailed. And though you pay for the super-premium wash, the heat of the day makes the faint smell of regurgitated milk waft to your nostrils as you drive to get industrial-strength cleaner, which you hope will remove your daughter's latest masterpiece from the wall in the spare bedroom. Either way, all the money you're spending makes you feel like you may evacuate the fettuccine Alfredo you had for lunch.

## CTFD

Roll up that vintage 1976 wool rug from the thrift store. Pack away that limited-edition movie figurine given to you by your college roommate. The antique chairs your parents passed down to you in the hopes they would one day be passed on to their grandchild, well, that succession stops with you, unless splintered furniture is the new trend.

If there's anything you cherish *more* than your child, put it away. Lock it in a metal box high on a shelf. Just keep in mind, your kid might not be able to open that box, but she'll get hold of it and throw it into a wall or at your head or something.

There's simply no way around it—your kid will destroy stuff. There are entire blogs and coffee table books dedicated to this truism. So getting mad about it proves about as useful and worthy as screaming at the moon. And once your tot shoves a peanut butter and jelly sandwich into your new Blu-ray player, if you don't keep some perspective, you'll go stark raving mad and end up screaming at the moon anyway.

*Preschoolers*

# DEVELOPMENT

## MY BOY LIKES GIRL TOYS

Your son got a Bat Cave playset from the grandparents for his birthday. It has an elevator, a Bat Computer, and a little holding cell to keep Gotham's worst villains off the streets. It lacks a Batman, however, because your son feels like Tinkerbell is the hero Gotham deserves.

Yes, Peter Pan's minuscule sidekick flies in and out of the hideout, spreading pixie dust and fighting crime. If that's where your son's obsession with the wee fairy ended, you'd probably stop worrying.

But he also wants to dress as Tinkerbell for his preschool dress-up day and wear the outfit to the family dinner next weekend. You run through all the possible insults his classmates could throw at him. And you try to land on the perfect way to tell your father that his grandson desperately wants to wear a green tube dress and sparkly wings.

And forget the potentially awkward conversation held while chewing on grilled chicken breast at your parents' dining room table. Here's a larger issue: Does your son's obsession with Tinkerbell mean he's gay? If so, how should that affect your parenting? Should you familiarize yourself with the Barbra Streisand catalog?

You stare at your son as he makes Tinkerbell clobber the Joker and wonder if he'll ever be a happy adult with a fairy as a hero.

 **CTFD**

To your son, Tinkerbell is neither a girl's character nor a boy's character. She's just a character, and a cool one at that. She can fly, she fights for what she wants, and she helped Peter Pan best Captain Hook. She's as much a hero as Batman, and she doesn't need a mask and a belt full of gadgets to win the day.

Kids don't know anything of gender. They just enjoy dressing up. Commercials, magazines, movies—all those things will ram typical gender roles into their heads soon enough. Let them enjoy playing without that barrier while they can. (Tell *that* to your dad.)

Oh, and you don't parent a gay child any different than any other child. So if you're truly concerned your son might be gay: 1. Get over it, and 2. Tinkerbell won't make him any more or less gay than he already is.

## MY CHILD REFUSES TO INTERACT WITH OTHERS

Any attempt to get your daughter to engage others at a playdate results in whining followed by her occupying a quiet corner where she can color in peace. It's as if she were preparing for art school. And you're frustrated because you've seen her act perfectly open and welcoming before, even with people she didn't know. Like, she probably thought "stranger danger" was the name of a party DJ. But for some reason, your once outgoing child has bloomed into a delicate wallflower.

Of course, if *you're* around she wants to play with you. She cares not that you organized the playdate so you could have some adult interaction with the other parents, a conversation that didn't revolve around what a storybook prince does for a living or what to name her imaginary horse. (You suggested the regal name Gallant for her stallion while she went with the more pedestrian Baby Poopy. And you feel great shame that you spent twenty minutes during the playdate debating this choice with her, especially considering the steed doesn't actually exist.)

You encourage her to interact and remind her that she *knows* the other kids. But she just clings to your leg and hides behind her hair. No explanation or gentle coaxing can get her to relax and play with other kids.

You picture a life in which she never leaves your side and your relationship devolves into codependency. You ponder if she's too shy to attend a school dance when she's older—is it creepy to throw a makeshift prom at your house just for your family?

Some kids are outgoing, some are shy, and some switch back and forth as they grow. Heck, some switch back and forth before lunch. If you suspect your child might have a developmental disorder or autism spectrum disorder, certainly raise that concern with your pediatrician. But you know your kid. Some just remain painfully shy, and there's nothing wrong with that. That said, if you're sure it's a phase, keep presenting scenarios in which she has the opportunity to act more outgoing. Don't force her, but rather let her reach that confidence level on her own. And repetition helps, so make a regular playdate with the same kids, but keep them short.

Of course, if you're social with the other parents at the playdate, she'll see you as an example. So don't feel like you need to hang out with her while she hides away. None of this means you shouldn't have a prom at your house anyway, though, because that sounds awesome.

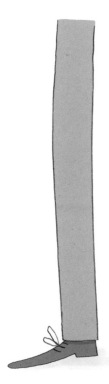

## MY CHILD HAS POTTY ACCIDENTS

Your preschooler already reads. OK, he's not reading *The Corrections* or even *Encyclopedia Brown and the Case of the Slippery Salamander*, but he can muddle his way through *Go, Dog. Go!* So tackling *Ulysses* can't be that far off. Yet despite this academic achievement, he can't seem to grasp the idea that he shouldn't pee in his pants.

You're flummoxed as to why your child, who's so advanced academically, falls so far behind in what you consider the number-one most important developmental milestone. Well, number one *and* number two, if you know what I mean.

Now that he's officially a kid and eating real food like meatloaf and baked beans, those poops are so much more . . . adult than they were in infancy. And forget the hygiene issue for a moment. You can't address this aggressively because then he may develop issues. You know, *weird* issues. You don't know exactly what those issues are, but you're sure they're the kind that lead to him adorning the office of the motel where he works with his unique taxidermy projects.

Besides, you really need to get online and see if they make diapers for teenagers because if he doesn't figure this out soon, he'll surely squish uncomfortably through his adolescence, smelling like a chicken ranch and gathering flies.

 **CTFD**

Though you shouldn't ignore potty accidents, they're perfectly common for kids as old as four or five, even six, especially boys. To help overcome this, find a tactic to which your child responds. Despite what you've probably been told, a reward system works well and won't create a twenty-year-old who thinks he deserves a prize for taking a dump in the toilet. (But the reward should be something small, like a sticker, not an Xbox.) You can also try a potty schedule: every thirty or sixty minutes, take the kid to the bathroom whether he needs to go or not. It'll help him learn to listen to his body. While you're at it, pass along this sage advice from my father-in-law: "Never trust a fart."

# MY CHILD HATES THE HIGH CHAIR

When you put your daughter in the high chair, she screams and refuses any food. You'd compare her to Regan from *The Exorcist*, but even that demonically possessed child was a better communicator.

She wants out of the high chair. You try to distract her. You jiggle her favorite doll in front of her, you make an elaborate balloon animal (aiming for a giraffe, you create something more like a uterus), and you dance an energetic jig that causes you to hurt something deep inside your leg—almost certainly a torn ligament.

But your little girl will have none of it. She'd rather give you her interpretation of wild chimpanzees battling each other over a tree branch. Her volume and emotional commitment to the theatrics escalate from vaudevillian to Broadway levels. And as she shakes her head back and forth, swatting away spoonfuls of mashed prunes, you begin to think she may actually rock the high chair right over, which would make the fits and tears suddenly relevant.

You don't understand why she wouldn't want to eat. On your list of favorite things to do, eating falls right after sleeping and just before more sleeping.

## CTFD

Awww. Your little one is exerting her independence. How sweet. And annoying.

To quell these types of outbursts, try compromises such as, "We can't play now, but let's eat first and we can play afterwards" or, "If we get through this bowl of Cheerios, I'll let you watch me cry for a while." Or if you frown on bribery like most, simply end the feeding, which will help reinforce that the high chair is used during mealtime. And you'll know when your child is actually big enough to not need a high chair.

When one of our kids protested his high chair, we faced him away from the group until he calmed down. Essentially it was a moment for the offender to chill out, or, if you prefer to go for more Amish nomenclature, it was a shunning. The tactic showed our son it's not an effective method of communication. At the very least, it would point his mouth—the source of the noise—in the other direction.

# MY CHILD LASHES OUT WHEN UPSET

There's something almost romantic about the image of the emotional artist. You know the type—brooding, smart, creative, struggling to express that perfect image or poem. But when that artist's chosen medium is Crayola and he has yet to master even coloring inside the lines, the outbursts that accompany those emotions seem less justified.

When he was an infant, you dealt with his fits by distracting him, but he's older now and, though it's tempting and totally possible, you can't simply overpower a preschooler. Now, like an eccentric sculptor or an impulsive writer, your child expresses his aggravation in egotistical bursts of physicality, complete with tears, shouting, and hurled objects. He flies into a whiny rage over a dropped carrot, an unjustly scheduled nap time, or a dearth of clean blue cups. And heaven forbid the latest episode of *Bubble Guppies* fails to record. Such unfairness could result in a tantrum that lasts longer than the show itself.

You try to convince him whatever's bothering him doesn't really matter. Yet your son reacts to negative emotions in a way only justified by a lackluster opening at a postmodern impressionist gallery.

## —————————— CTFD ——————————

Try this perspective: whatever set him off doesn't matter to *you*. To him, it's the worst thing since the Beatles broke up. Unlike the outbursts of an infant, which are usually exacerbated by a lack of language, your preschooler's tantrums are aggravated by not having the tools to deal with his disappointment, anger, sadness, and other feelings emo kids thrive on. Though you've probably offered suggestions (such as counting to ten, doing a silly body shake, or asking him to draw a picture of what he's mad at, then jumping on it), he clearly hasn't perfected the skill. After all, you can't give a chimp a hammer and expect it to build you a gazebo. Not that your child resembles a chimp . . . Well, maybe the ears.

Anyway, when he begins to fly into a tantrum, remind him of the methods for expressing emotions that don't involve throwing a storybook into the wall. Eventually he'll get it and be able to focus the energy toward coping with what's bothering him. And you can remove drywall spackling paste from your weekly shopping list.

## MY CHILD SHOWS NO INTEREST IN LEARNING

You have nothing against Spider-Man costumes or Hot Wheels cars. If educational milestones employed these and other toys, your son's accomplishments would secure his place at the head of the class. He'd probably sit there on a throne he made from intricately assembled Lego bricks.

Unfortunately, the folks who make such decisions about children and their achievements tend to use more dated and quantifiable methods such as proficiency in reading or art. And your boy shows as much interest in those pursuits as a Bobak marmot shows in chamber music.

Unlike the child who struggles with topics, yours simply doesn't care to learn. While other kids find joy in learning their letters and numbers, your child would rather run screaming through the backyard for the better part of the afternoon. You find phonics books to help him learn to read, you show him how to draw a house using basic shapes, you even ask him to count the slices of apple on his plate in the hopes that it could be considered math.

You try everything you can to generate some interest— you plead, bargain, shout, and bribe. Nothing works. Grasping for any sign of an interest in education, you convince yourself that the spaceship he makes out of wooden blocks means he might excel in engineering.

---------------- **CTFD** ----------------

Believe it or not, he's learning academics while he plays. Building a Hot Wheels track for a car to roll down involves physics. Creating a tunnel with Lego bricks involves geometry. This doesn't mean your son is Stephen Hawking just because he bounces a ball down the stairs. But you can find academic lessons in every activity. Help him with a Lego set and have him count out the pieces he needs. When playing Star Wars, discuss real space travel or lasers. Eventually he will show an interest in the regular academic issues. Once he starts to make the connection between things like math and piloting a jet or reading and archeology, he'll invest even more. And later in his life, he won't be fazed when you tell him you're stealing his Halloween candy to teach him about dietary criminology.

# MY CHILD ISN'T AS TALL AS OTHER KIDS

The mother you used to chat with while dropping off at day care wants to reconnect, so you schedule a playdate for your kids. When she shows up, her child looks tall enough to be her designated driver.

You've always felt your girl lagged behind others when it came to growth rate, but this visit confirms something is amiss. It's especially odd because your daughter is three months older than hers. You assume the rapid growth has something to do with a job she must have at the racetrack. The kid's obviously gotten into some horse steroids or something.

As the playdate winds to a close with no display of horse-like behavior at all, you realize her kid stands a half-foot taller than yours because of better genetics. Until that moment, you never knew your genes were deficient. Yet here stands her statuesque child, who makes yours look like a tiny freak in a traveling carnival sideshow.

A visit to the pediatrician confirms your daughter falls in the average range for height and weight. Your concerns, however, continue to fester. You offer up more milk than usual, you pile dinner plates high with food rich in calcium and vitamin D. When she wants a cookie, you hold it just out of reach so she has to stretch to get it. At night, you sneak into her room and pull on her legs.

 **CTFD**

Just as your child hits developmental milestones at her own pace, so does her physical body. Some kids grow slower than others. And some kids grow so fast, each time you see them you think the parents must have traded in their old kid for a new one at some sort of black market child exchange. Maintain your regular medical checkup schedule and your pediatrician will let you know if the rate of growth is abnormally slow. Or you could simply monitor it yourself by doing the classic growth chart in the doorway. Most kids grow eventually, and when they do, you'll miss when they were little and weep as you look at the little growth chart in the doorway.

# MY CHILD DOESN'T KNOW THE ALPHABET

Your daughter's preschool classmate can already recite the whole alphabet and she's two months younger than your child. Her mother proudly asks her to say the letters at each playdate and she does so with a sweet smile, the braggart. Big deal, *you* know the alphabet, and at one point in your life you also knew how to diagram a sentence. Ask that little girl to throw out some diphthongs and watch her crumble.

People tend to frown on destroying the will of a preschooler, however, so you take a more positive approach. You work on the alphabet with your daughter over dinner, after her nap, in the morning before preschool, and while clipping her toenails. You sing variations of the "Alphabet Song" on the chance that she might like country more than pop, or perhaps she's into reggae. You purchase alphabet picture books, CDs, blocks, magnets, and flashcards. You begin to critique the learning tools. Aren't there any X words other than xylophone? Does that flipbook really show a narwhal for the letter N? That's pretentious.

Though your daughter shows no improvement, you could now literally say the alphabet backward. Speaking of backward, your daughter seems to have regressed. When she once could get all the way to P without stumbling, now she can't even get to H. And the last time you asked her to run through it, you thought she might have mumbled a number and, somehow, drawn a hieroglyph of a cat. Without mastering the most fundamental building blocks of communication and education, you fear your beloved daughter is doomed to a life of dining at places with pictures on the menu.

### CTFD

Your daughter will get it. Just as with other developmental stages, all kids learn the alphabet at their own rate. Continue to work with her, but don't overwhelm her. Pressuring her to memorize it could turn her away from the task. And talk to her teacher, if she has one, about how they're learning in class. It'll help you decide whether to reinforce that method at home or try something else. Overall, your most important task is to be patient. And your next most important task is explaining that L-M-N-O is not a word. I didn't learn that until my sophomore year of college.

# BEHAVIOR

# MY CHILD THROWS A FIT WHEN HE DOESN'T GET HIS WAY

Your caring, cooing son learned to walk and has a good grip on language. He's finally showing that independence for which you eagerly waited. And now he thinks he owns the damn place, making the tremendous leap from sweet child to Kaiser Wilhelm II.

You've tried to reason with him, telling him it doesn't work that way. You offer evidence, like the fact that you graduated from high school and can walk all the way to the store and back and *you* don't even own the place. But it doesn't register. Worse still, if you don't agree that a Popsicle at 7 am makes a perfectly fine breakfast, you're assaulted with a mighty tantrum.

Screw backroom deals, screw diplomacy. There's no more effective way to achieve what you want than screaming, crying, kicking, and flailing. (I'm not up on my history, but I believe this is the exact tactic used by Kaiser Wilhelm II.) Your son knows this because you see only one way out, one way to make it stop—give in. Hand over the Popsicle and try to convince yourself it counts as a helping of fruit.

You weep tears of submission as he wipes melted yellow goo on your face and neck. And you don't dare try to stop him, because if you do, another tantrum awaits.

 **CTFD**

It's hard, because after a long day, a toddler's tantrum seems as pleasant as being strapped into a chair while Elmo leans over you chewing tin foil. But if you react too negatively—or worse, cave in—over time, your son will learn to do it to get his way.

Keep in mind your son's not being an jerk ... on purpose. You need to teach him things like patience, empathy, gratitude, and that you need to wait for your paycheck to clear before you buy that pirate playset.

So when he starts to throw a fit, speak calmly. Explain that he can't have what he wants right now, but also offer a compromise. If he continues, go ahead and try an appropriate consequence, or simply leave the room for a bit. It will remove you from his equation and also offer you some time to cool off. Or strap him into a chair while Elmo leans over him chewing tin foil.

*Behavior*

## MY CHILD DISOBEYS ME

You set boundaries in the home. Far from unreasonable, they exist to help maintain order—no climbing on the counter, no snacks before dinner, no boosting the neighbor's car for a joyride. These rules are clear. In fact, if they were any more clear birds would fly into them.

Yet, while your precious daughter knows the rules well enough to repeat them back to you, she willfully disobeys you at every opportunity. Leave the room to grab a glass of water and you get a panicked call from Tim next door saying your little girl just peeled off down the street in his Hyundai Sonata. This combination of defiance, bravado, and ignorance might make for an excellent career as a reality television star.

To confirm that this behavior signifies active disobedience, you warn her not to go down the playground slide headfirst. She makes eye contact with you, lies on her belly, and rockets down the incline with her devilish grin leading the way. If preschoolers wore white gloves, she'd have removed one and slapped you across the face with it.

 **CTFD**

Contrary to the way my wife plays pool, rules were *not* made to be broken. You surely told your daughter why you have these rules, but if you did that while chastising her for breaking them, it may not have fully registered. She saw it as a scolding, not an explanation.

Take a moment when you're not freaking out to readdress the family rules and why they exist. Respond with a consequence the *first* time she breaks a rule, not after a warning. Also, we all need to feel the victory of winning an argument occasionally. Look for opportunities for her to get her way, like, maybe let her have a snack before dinner every once in a while. As long as you explain it's not the norm, she'll feel a bit of freedom and power that could placate her and keep her from hotwiring the McConnells' station wagon down the block.

Still, the law of averages means you'll probably have a "teachable moment" with her soon, a parent's way of saying "I told you so." As satisfying as this moment will feel, you just want to keep her from breaking an arm, or at least stop her from leaving skidmarks on the street outside of your house.

# NO PUNISHMENT SEEMS TO WORK ON MY CHILD

When it comes to punishing bad behavior, no options remain. You've tried time-outs, you've tried removing privileges, you've even tried getting rid of certain beloved toys, but nothing gets through to your child. You swore you'd never spank, but you're starting to realize this standoff might come down to a swat on the *tuchus*, perhaps with a rowing oar. What else could you possibly do?

Punishment, after all, teaches children right from wrong and how to be good people. If you don't address this complete disregard for common decency, soon the kids will take over. Oh, you'll have order in your house—a primitive order run by your untamed offspring. You won't need an excuse to get out of that playdate you weren't so excited about, not when you're tied to the fridge with knitting yarn as your feral child dances around you, jabbing his makeshift Nerf spear skyward.

You use the Le Creuset wine opener to cut yourself free and make a mad dash for the door. As you flee, you find a pig's head on a spike in the hallway, and a broken conch shell in the living room. Behind you, you hear them coming. They want to hunt you down. The savagery won't end until the whole place erupts in flames. And you're not certain your homeowner's insurance covers "child uprising."

———————————— **CTFD** ————————————

Children test boundaries. Stick with it, be patient. Eventually he'll figure out the full meaning of the punishments you dole out, especially when he realizes that Thomas train you put on the top shelf of the storage closet really won't be back for a week.

And don't forget the power of positive reinforcement. Showing how much you appreciate good behavior often works better than punishing when he misbehaves. I don't mean you need to buy him a new bike just for putting his shoes on when you asked him to. Keep it simple. When things are going smoothly and he's accommodating, thank him. Maybe throw him a high-five, if you're the type of family that high-fives.

For the record, we are not always a high-fiving family nor do we fist bump, but we do toss up the rock-and-roll forked fingers gesture often. This is, of course, much to the chagrin of *my* parents.

# MY CHILD ACTS UNSAFELY AROUND ANIMALS

Your house is a very, very, very fine house, with two cats in the yard that you fear your child will tackle like a linebacker.

You imagined an idyllic family complete with a menagerie of pets, but your daughter thinks animals are nothing more than fully automated toys that never run out of batteries. She pets them aggressively, uses them as pillows, and tests their patience in ways that make you want to ask the Pope if a Persian tabby can be nominated for sainthood.

And when someone passes walking their dog, your kid runs up and rubs noses with the strange canine. Each time, you yank her back by her sweatshirt just as the other person yanks back on the leash. You warn her that she must approach animals cautiously and first check with the owner if it's OK, lest the pup make a treat of her nose.

A timid dog lashing out sounds bad, but when your daughter says she'd like to climb inside a pen at the zoo's safari exhibit on her next visit, you realize the full potential of the danger. After all, how will you ever show your face in the monthly book club meeting when all the other members know you let you daughter get attacked by a Bengal tiger?

After canceling your zoo membership you turn your efforts to the most domestic problem. You must find a way to keep her from ending up as Fido's chew toy.

─────────────── **CTFD** ───────────────

The good news is, she probably freaks out around pets because she loves animals. If she won't listen to you, go to an expert. No, I don't mean a parenting expert. I mean an animal expert.

Go to a petting zoo, farm, or ranch—someplace where she can closely interact with a professional animal handler. They'll probably cover the same ground as you (don't get in the animal's face, let them smell your hand, etc.), but sometimes your daughter just needs to hear it from someone who doesn't also make her baloney sandwiches.

The only other solution is to dress like a bear and jump from her closet late at night. That will cure her love of strange animals and also distinguish her as the only white-haired child in her class.

# MY CHILD DOES NOT UNDERSTAND CONSEQUENCES

The concept of "cause and effect" seems simple enough. Warmth melts ice, for example, so the tub of Rocky Road left on the counter now holds nothing but sweet soup. Or if your son slides down the stairs on a couch cushion, he'll knock over the decorative vase on the landing, which, in turn, makes you so mad you pop a blood vessel in your eye, which means you'll look like some sort of demonic bog creature on date night. See? Cause and effect . . . and effect and effect.

Not only does your child fail to grasp this most pedestrian of correlations, but he also refuses to equate bad behavior with any form of punishment. Whether you're from the school of thought that refrains from typical retribution (such as time-outs or removed privileges) or the group that believes in exercising the parental version of the nuclear option (tossing his Disney DVDs out the window and blowing his college fund in Vegas), your child's inability to see the link between a transgression and a fitting resolution flummoxes you.

When you do sit him down for a talk or some other consequence, he genuinely doesn't understand why. You explain to him, "I told you not to squirt the bottle of mustard all over the place or you'd be in trouble." But as the swirl of yellow condiment drips down the closet door, he demonstrates exacerbation at your response. You warn him that police do not respond so warmly to such displays of incredulousness, nor do they appreciate depictions of a rocket flying to the moon crafted from sandwich toppings.

## CTFD

He'll come around. This is one of those issues where you simply have to be consistent. You're dealing with an unpleasant mix of exploration, learning, and, I guess, sheer solipsism.

Repetition will drive it home. Also, kids test boundaries in multiple ways and at various times in their development (see also: grade school, high school, college, adulthood). Chances are he *does* understand bad behavior warrants some sort of punishment, but he just wants to see how consistent that is while exploring his mustard craft.

# PARENTING STYLES & SKILLS

# ATTACHMENT PARENTING

Attachment parenting sounded like the perfect technique with which to raise your daughter. You have a boundless supply of love to offer, and the idea of a heightened level of attention to your baby fits your personality. You thought it would also help sculpt the ideal relationship with your child, one that went beyond the typical bond shared by most parents and kids, one that would serve as a shimmering beacon to all about the power of love and the joy of parenthood.

Only you feel like you're drowning in a sea of neediness. And while attending to your whiny child hour after hour, all you can think about is when you can have a martini.

You try to adhere to the principles of attachment parenting, to maintain emotional availability and awareness for your child. But sometimes you just want to be away from her. More so, you want to jump on a steamer ship and venture solo to Belize. And while co-sleeping looks adorable in ads, you can only take so many kicks to the neck from your baby's pudgy leg before you start pining for an isolation tank that locks from the inside.

 **CTFD**

You're not a failure because you need some space every once in a while. No, you're just a regular person. Go ahead and have that martini.

If you don't allow yourself some private time now and again, you may snap and one day find yourself in a heated debate with a shopping cart while wearing a soup pot on your head. (Even the principles of attachment parenting call for "balance in your personal life" to prevent any negative effects.)

If attachment parenting works for you, have at it. And there are plenty of community groups out there who can help you when you have trouble. But don't force a technique that doesn't work for you or your baby. Try different techniques—or cherry-pick things from a handful of techniques—and see what you and your baby respond to best.

Of course, you could always just CTFD. Just sayin'.

# MINIMALIST PARENTING

You didn't want to overload your kids with activities, and you prefer to let things in your house play out with a more relaxed schedule. Playdates happen if and when convenient. Extracurricular activities occur sometimes, probably, maybe. And those tilapia fillets in the fridge might go to waste if not cooked today, but your little guy really wants hot dogs again. And hot dogs are awesome anyway, right?

He has the time and space to entertain himself, to play and grow on his own. And you have time to chill out. You see the other moms and dads going gray under the stress of maintaining a busy schedule. By comparison, you're as mellow as a hemp farmer at a drum circle.

But when your mom calls in a panic because she's locked herself out of the house and she probably left the iron on, you need to hustle. You rush to get dressed, but your child can't be found. The last you checked in on him, he was quietly building a racetrack for his cars. When was that, Tuesday? You finally find him at the neighbor's house, where he's been secretly living for a week.

You beg him to get his shoes on and he lollygags through the task, eventually completing it in a mere thirty minutes. You feel your cool exterior start to crack, and as he slowly moseys to the car, you shout at him to hurry up. The outburst stuns him so much that he collapses to the ground, further delaying your departure. In the distance, you hear fire truck sirens wailing as they barrel toward the smoking husk that was once your mom's house.

 **CTFD**

Allowing your child time to relax and play can have numerous benefits, but you still need to be present in your child's life. Minimalist parenting means "don't overload your schedule," not "stop parenting." (Same with CTFD, by the way.) Your kid still needs to know how to get to school on time, that painting the cat purple is a no-no, and that you aren't just a piece of furniture that combs his hair from time to time.

# TIGER MOTHER PARENTING

You read *Battle Hymn of the Tiger Mother* and thought Amy Chua's emotionally aggressive technique seemed like a refreshingly shocking alternative to the gaggle of attachment parents and minimalist parents fussing around the playground. You've always gone against the grain, anyway. You're bold, you're daring. You even have a tattoo.

So you apply Chua's technique. You hand Mother's Day cards back to your daughter, saying they aren't good enough. You keep playdates to a minimum. Your love remains a gift given only when your kid makes monumental achievements in school, such as inventing an engine that runs on wastewater. And strangely, because of all this, your child hates you.

You tell yourself it's OK that your daughter seems emotionally detached from you. Your face may adorn a dartboard in her room, but at least she's excelling in school. So you might never meet the grandkids and no one comes to your funeral. So what? As long as she's getting straight-As on her report card, you're going to stick with it.

Tigers, after all, don't snuggle on the couch. Tigers don't get warm hugs from their daughters. Hugs are overrated, anyway.

 **CTFD**

For the record, the fervor over Chua's book failed to present the entire story, which was a memoir, not a how-to. In the years following the release of *Battle Hymn of the Tiger Mother*, Chua even admitted some of her parenting tactics were wrong. And a study by the University of Texas showed Tiger Mother parenting actually produces the opposite of the intended effect—children get lower grades and are prone to depression. So, like a *real* tiger, let your instincts guide you. If your child seems to respond to positive reinforcement, use it. If she likes to be left alone to attempt tasks, do that. And *that* method is just called "parenting."

Besides, you shouldn't keep tigers in the house.

## HELICOPTER PARENTING

At the playground, you're always within arm's reach of your son. When he goes out to ride his bike, you encase him in armor and make sure he never goes faster than a common garden slug (and, of course, you're at his side the whole time). During his schoolmate's birthday party, you keep him from climbing the tree with his other friends. This saves him from possible injury and also makes you more environmentally friendly than the other parents.

You're a helicopter parent and you see no shame in that. You don't want your son to get hurt. So you're always close in case he falls or trips or even looks like he might sneeze. In the rare moments when you're not hovering around him, you spend your time searching the internet for a suit made of Nerf that might fit him.

When he does stumble and miss your grasp, he goes into an inconsolable crying jag that justifies your protection. While his boo-boo might look like nothing more than a tiny bloodless scrape, judging by his reaction, it's clearly a serious injury. As you debate running him to the emergency room to remove any doubts about broken bones or other internal damage, you cradle him in your arms, silently cursing yourself for not saving him from this horrible accident. You vow to double your efforts and start work on building your own child-sized Nerf suit.

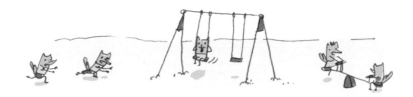

Bumps, bruises, scrapes, and cuts hurt. But if your child never experiences them, he'll never learn to differentiate between the ones he can shake off and the ones that deserve an inconsolable crying jag.

One of the toughest things a parent must do is allow a child to take physical risks and, yes, occasionally fail at them. Helicopter parents often compound the problem of overreacting to injuries by doing the same thing when they scoop their child up to coddle and panic. (Fun Fact: Coddle & Panic is also the name of a popular folk duo from the late 1940s.*)

So be safe—some consoling is great, but don't overdo it. If you can walk off the pain of a stubbed toe, so can he. He'll end up having a lot more fun. And consider this: I once met a dad at the playground who admitted he was overprotective. I thought he was joking because we were laughing about our parenting failures. A few minutes later, I saw him pushing his son on the swing. He was so scared his six-year-old would get hurt he was barely pushing him. Like, literally, the boy hardly moved. He looked miserable. And that child was Dick Cheney.**

*Not true.

**Also not true.

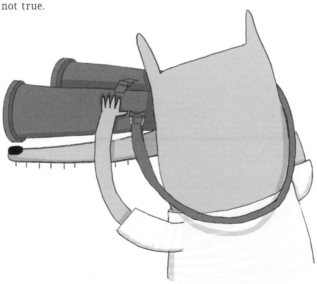

## PERMISSIVE PARENTING

You tend to handle things as they come. If your daughter shouts in a restaurant, you bribe her with ice cream to occupy her mouth. If she wants to stay up past her bedtime to watch the end of *Cinderella*, you allow it. It just makes things easier than enduring another tantrum.

Only things aren't easier. She gets even more demanding with each passing week. And when you do try to draw the proverbial line in the sandbox, she stomps across it, throws that sand in your face, and launches into an epic fit that rattles windows and sets off car alarms.

You also notice she doesn't interact well with other kids. She insists on making up rules that benefit her during whatever game is played and purposefully interrupts other kids' activities. When she doesn't get her way on the playground, she pushes the other kids or yells at them. It all seems so weird to you since you never behave that way . . . well, except for that one semester you spent in Florence, but everyone experimented back then.

To get her to behave nicer to the other kids, you offer a stop at the toy store on the way home if she demonstrates better behavior. To your pleasure, it works and only costs you $40. You do some quick math in your head and determine that, at that daily rate, the price of making her behave like a decent person as she grows into adulthood will only run roughly $198,000.

Though you might not know it, you're what's called a Permissive Parent. That's shorthand for "you've spoiled your kid too much." In an effort to minimize confrontations with your daughter, you've essentially taught her that she can get whatever she wants if she just makes enough noise. And while that technique may work when you're, say, lost in a cave, it's not great for learning empathy.

But it's not too late. Steel yourself and prepare for a few confrontations. Actually, prepare for a bunch and stand your ground. It's going to get loud. Don't return the volume, though. Stay levelheaded and calm.

Boundaries help your child grow mentally and emotionally. So you'll need to impose boundaries to which you stick. Also, you should explain why they exist. She can't have popcorn while you're at the market because it'll spoil her lunch. She can't yank the doll out of Tina's hands because we're sharing. She can't spray-paint her name on the wall by school because it's against the law. Eventually your child will grow to understand she can't always get her way and why. And it won't cost you anything, unless you want to invest in some of those *Scared Straight* videos for good measure.

*Parenting Styles & Skills*

# I HAVEN'T KEPT UP WITH CPR TRAINING

At the pre-birth CPR class, you saw a lot of expectant couples bearing the same weary face as you—the one that comes from information overload combined with mounting panic. Most brains shut off when they reach capacity, but parents-to-be like you keep cramming stuff in. More classes, more brochures, more advice. And you have to. Should the need arise at crunch time, you don't want to be the person who forgot how to do a "Full Moon" birth position.

Once the CPR class ends, you feel a sense of accomplishment so powerful, you tell yourself it's all right to skip some of the required maintenance. You know you're supposed to practice CPR on a throw pillow, but that feels as goofy as it sounds.

And now that the tyke has arrived, you've faced sleep deprivation, puréed peas, first steps, and every other exhausting thing parenthood brings. So you put practicing on the backburner, though you're starting to forget the steps. Is it check for blockage, then tilt the head back, or tilt the head back, then check for blockage? And you can't remember if deep knee bends are supposed to be involved or if they're part of the weekend workout you also jettisoned when the baby arrived. Even when things have calmed down and you feel more rested, there's almost nothing more unappealing than spending a date night blowing into the mouth of a creepy rubber baby.

Choking can't be as common as people say, right? It must be a racket cooked up by Big CPR—the manufacturers of instructional pamphlets and fake babies. You've grown to resent the CPR instructors and professionals who you imagine would look at you disapprovingly for not practicing. No, you won't let yourself get bullied into sitting in a room at the community center for an entire afternoon practicing for a scenario that'll never happen. *¡Viva la independencia!*

There are many, many things parents are told they must do that they don't have to—show vocabulary flashcards to your baby, limit your toddler's TV time, help him with homework, don't help him with homework, hold off on teaching him to juggle power drills until he's at least six years old. But one of the only things you *actually* have to do is keep up with your CPR classes. Because should the need arise at crunch time, nobody wants to be the person who forgot how to do CPR. So take the class and CTFD. And you need to do it once before you give birth, once a year later, then every two years until your children grow old and retire. Our orange shag Polyfill pillows were saved over and over.

And we've actually had to use CPR on a child. Twice. And after each time, my wife had to use it on me after my heart stopped.

# PARENTHOOD

# I'M NOT THE TYPE OF PARENT I THOUGHT I'D BE

You thought you were going to be that cool parent—you know, the one that all the other parents admire for having it so together. With a unique blend of techniques and other tools, you expected to set a standard by which all others would judge themselves. Yes, in your little Rat Pack of moms and dads, you were going to be the Frank Sinatra.

Instead, you're more like Joey Bishop.

All the research, all the planning, and all the exercises you did in preparation for parenthood proved about as useful as the fondue pot gathering dust on the top shelf of your kitchen hutch. This parenting thing is nothing like you expected. Rather than handling challenges with grace and humor, you usually resort to yelling and, though the memory is hazy, you may have once thrown an entire Barbie playset in the trash as a punishment.

In your most clear moments, you understand the way this must affect your child. Your master plan wasn't just about you, after all. As a result of your lackluster parenting, your kid won't excel in school and will probably have no friends thanks to the host of mental issues with which you've saddled her. At least you've given your child the slowly blossoming inspiration for a career as an exotic dancer.

 **CTFD**

First, what's your issue with exotic dancers? They're perfectly fine people.

Second, as a parent, you will screw up. A lot. There's no way to avoid it, so just accept that you won't ever attain Flawless Parent status. The good news is you're not alone, and one mistake (or even an unbroken series of seemingly disastrous mistakes) does not mean you've done irrevocable damage.

No one can predict what parenting brings or how it'll affect you. It tests everything you've learned before and adds an unquantifiable amount of stress. Seriously, it's like boot camp without the marching. And other parents, even the ones who appear to you like the Frank Sinatra in your Rat Pack, flail just as much as you do. I'm not saying that yelling all the time is OK. But when it comes to parenting, we're all Joey Bishop.

# I DON'T PLAN ON TAKING PATERNITY LEAVE

There's a baby on the way and you're about to be a proud papa. Congrats, dude. It's a blast—a *challenging* blast, but a blast nonetheless.

But perhaps you're not going to take advantage of your company's paternity leave. Your DNA and that imitation leather briefcase scream at you to get back to work. You are a provider, after all, and must supply sustenance (or at least money for Chinese takeout) for your family.

You're sure that a couple of days spent at home after you get back from the hospital will provide enough of the poop-and-sleeplessness experience. Those papers aren't going to push themselves. And if you don't make an appearance in the office at least every nine days or so, Jake from accounting will probably steal your stash of Post-It Notes.

Besides, you don't want to make it seem to your employer that you don't care about work. In fact, most men don't use all of their paternity leave for that very reason. And data shows most employers think men who take paternity leave don't care about their job as much as those who don't take any leave.

There, see? I just backed up your reasoning. You must not linger in the home, despite the fact that you'll miss a series of amazing milestones and a great swath of your child's first few weeks or months on this planet. No, you are a provider and must provide.

## CTFD

If you're lucky enough to work for a company that offers paternity leave, take it. All of it. If you think your employer will assume that means you care more about family than work, talk with your supervisor. Discuss your concerns and explain you do care about work, but this is an important time for you to be home.

And if they don't get it, spend a portion of your paternity leave looking for another job, because your employer is a sack of donkey balls. You'll be happier either way.

# I DON'T ALWAYS LIKE MY CHILD

The word "love" doesn't accurately capture the feeling you have for your son. You want the word to shine brilliantly, tower greatly, sing angelically, and inspire powerfully. Your love for your child makes other loves feel shame for not loving so monumentally. And yet, sometimes you don't *like* your kid.

When he refuses to wash his hands after going to the bathroom, then lies to you about doing it, it's bad enough. But things really get bad when he does this and then insists on sharing your sandwich ... and you only find out about the failure to cleanse afterward. The ensuing discussion becomes a shouting match and at some point you realize if this were a roommate in college you'd have booted him out by now or at least put his hand in a bowl of warm water while he was sleeping.

This emotional dichotomy confuses you. Even for a fleeting moment, disliking your own child highlights a deficiency and a pettiness in you. Maybe you were never meant to be a parent. Maybe you should've stuck with cats. You like cats. And cats never get their poopy hands all over your turkey club.

————————————— CTFD —————————————

Just as with your best friend (and even your cat), you may have disagreements with your child that make you want to walk away for a while. Do exactly that. It doesn't make you a bad parent. In fact, it makes you a smart one.

However you blow off steam—yoga, a jog, reading, painting, welding, clog dancing, macaroni art—take some time to chill out, especially so you refrain from saying or doing something hurtful. And remember that your son is still figuring things out and he needs your help to do that. So don't hold anything against him for too long. Upon your return, explain to him why you were upset and discuss ways to deal with it should it come up again.

And for the record, cats *never* wash their hands. So think about that, Judgey McJudgerton.

# I DON'T FEEL LIKE A DAD

When you first cradle your newborn in your arms after accompanying your wife through an exhausting delivery, you feel amazement, excitement, fear, accomplishment, and love. But you also feel confusion because, while you experience all those overwhelming emotions, you don't really feel like a father. Or rather, you don't immediately experience the cinematic love of your child displayed by dads in all of those heartfelt movies-of-the-week on basic cable.

Rather than doting on and cooing to your little one, primal instincts take over. You spend your first night in the neonatal wing hiding behind a blind you construct out of hospital gowns and a defibrillator, just waiting for a slow orderly to pass so you can spear her with an IV stand. Just as a nurse wanders by, you raise your weapon and lunge. Her shriek snaps you out of your delusion and you apologize for wearing a surgical mask as a loincloth.

After you bring your baby home, those primitive urges continue. That Evenflo Jump & Go exerciser looks like it's got too much slack. If your baby really gets going, he could knock his head against the doorway. You scurry to the hardware store and return with giant foam pads, screws, and washers. You make that doorway so safe, even a charging mastodon wouldn't get hurt bumping into it.

And though you still aren't connecting emotionally with your baby, you've completed the cave painting depicting your mighty conquests on the dining room wall using puréed carrots and blueberries. Those in neighboring caves will tell tales of your greatness.

Despite all the stories that suggest the arrival of a baby flips a magic switch that immediately makes us the best version of ourselves, that doesn't happen right away for everyone. (And many women experience the same delay.) So when you see your baby for the first time, that feeling of actually being a father might not sink in because, like a caveman, you're suddenly concerned with providing pelts and saber-toothed cat steaks. Once you're able to slow down and adapt to your new life, you'll let the chaos unfold, reveling in the absurd joy and cinematic love of fatherhood. And thanks to the butcher down the block, you won't injure yourself hunting for dinner.

# I GET EMOTIONAL ABOUT EVERYTHING

You love crime shows. If it starts with a murder, ends with a trial, and features a lot of graphic violence in between, you're happy.

Since having your girl, however, you see the victims, no matter how old, as former children. Fictional children, yes, but children nonetheless. They were once little folks like your daughter, and then they grew up, got mixed up with a jealous software magnate or media tycoon or drug dealer, and ended up dead. And that means their fictional parents will mourn them for the rest of their fictional lives.

Any story in which someone dies—a moody period film, a tense drama, even disaster films—you now see through the lens of parenthood. So while watching that apocalyptic spectacle, when the meteor hits Earth and sends a tsunami to shore, you weep for those families. Seriously, you might as well be watching *Sophie's Choice*.

Besides mourning all the fake people who've died for your enjoyment, you also mourn your love of that type of entertainment. You quietly spend your rare free time staring at the wall, because walls never die.

## CTFD

Being a parent makes you think about the stories people tell in a different way. The stakes are higher for every TV show, movie, book, play, and comic because every character was once a baby. This eventually wears off, but it could take a while. Like, a long while. By the way, this also applies to the news, which registers as even more tragic because it's real. Don't feel bad if you need to ignore current events for a while. You won't miss anything drastic. In fact, here's a ubiquitous newscast script you can read instead: "People are treating each other badly in various parts of the world. The weather will be seasonal. Now, here's a dog that plays the kazoo!"

In the meantime, your kid has welcomed a whole new genre back into your life: children's shows. The characters may seem odd, but no more so than a homicide detective with OCD. And, personally, I was more excited about that latest *Thomas & Friends* movie than my boys were.

I'm telling you, man, one day that Diesel 10 is going to push the steamies too far.

# I'M DEPRESSED

You're not happy. Instead, you feel like you're just triaging childcare all day and because of that you aren't able to enjoy parenting. You simply don't have time.

The need to take care of your child outweighs everything in your life and you feel trapped in a role for which you are ill-equipped. Even worse, you feel like your child is trapped just like you are, like she'd be better off with a parent who wasn't as stressed, as tired, as financially strapped, as depressed.

You snap at your partner. You weep over your girl's cute face when she wakes up late at night. You rage at the universe for not making you a better parent. You tell yourself you just need sleep and you'd be able to handle everything. Though you know regular sleep is a long way off.

 **CTFD**

You're not a bad parent. You're depressed, and not in the way that can be fixed with a few repeated listenings of Bauhaus's *Burning from the Inside*. And recent studies show that postpartum depression can occur in men, too. Other studies show depression in parents could have developmental effects on the child, such as a desire to play bass or write poetry about trees.

I battled depression while our boys were infants and I was a work-at-home dad. My wife encouraged me to seek help, which I did, and while it didn't solve everything, it gave me the tools I needed to help myself. (And I don't mean prescriptions, though that would've been rad.)

Seriously, though, seek professional help. There's nothing wrong with it. Talk things out with a therapist who'll help you learn some ways to cope with and hopefully overcome the effects of depression and stress. Listening to Bauhaus doesn't hurt either.

## MY PLANS ALWAYS GET RUINED

You organize a list of things to do while your child naps—prep dinner, clean out the junk drawer, pay bills, and return that email from Harriet about what wine to purchase for the weekend's potluck. You make sure not to load up the time with too many tasks, and thankfully you're rested, so you don't need to spend an hour staring mindlessly into a cup of coffee. Except nap time comes and your daughter won't sleep.

After a while, you just give up and plop her on the floor next to you in the living room. You attempt a few of the tasks, but she keeps trying to grab the bills from the stack, and you can't leave her to her own devices while you prep dinner. You tried that once and found her hanging from the curtain rod, pretending to be a mountain climber.

When you were in the workforce, you were great at handling crises as they arose. Projects would collapse at the last minute, people missed deadlines, clients canceled, leaving a hole in the budget, and programs crashed. You could deftly tackle any of it. In fact, you thrived on it. The difference is coworkers never screech at the top of their lungs. A missing file never cries uncontrollably. A blown deadline never refuses to eat its puréed green beans.

So no nap for your daughter means you won't complete these tasks and she'll act cranky during dinner. Basically, your day is blown. And you're out of wine.

 **CTFD**

One of the biggest adaptations you'll make is the ability to roll with the punches. For me, the adaptation has been a hard one, but I did it. (I wrote the preceding sentence in past tense, hoping that by the time this book comes out I'll have actually adapted. In truth, it still drives me batty.) So you'll undoubtedly get the hang of it.

You have to get comfortable with the fact that some or maybe all of the things you need to get done won't get done when you want (like writing a book, for example, but my kids couldn't care less about that). It just means that, rather than presenting your famous white bean chili, you might have to buy a Costco platter for the potluck (or ask the publisher to push back the deadline).

## I'M EMBARRASSED BY MY KID'S BEHAVIOR

Everyone in your family looks forward to Friday night. That's the night when you take your spouse and son to a favorite restaurant and enjoy a modest meal out in the real world. You sit down at the table and the server approaches to take your order. You've coached your son all week on how to politely order his own food. This is the big moment. He looks at the server and shouts, "PENIS! PENIS! PENIS!"

It doesn't stop there. When he's not boisterously screaming the names of private parts, he attempts to climb on the table, throws his crayons, and sings a perpetual loop of "Jingle Bells," though Christmas is seven months away. And this display is only the latest in a series of embarrassing moments. His manners have gone the way of his crayons.

Other patrons turn and stare. You hiss at him to stop, but that just encourages him to ramp up the body-part cheer, laughing the whole time. As far as he's concerned, he's a comedy genius on par with Shecky Greene. No amount of warnings, calming words, or threats has any effect. You smile sheepishly at the server as she rushes to fill your order, just so your son will have a grilled cheese to work on rather than this impromptu biology lesson.

You'd rather just avoid this embarrassment altogether. So when the server returns with your drinks, you ask if the restaurant delivers.

There is no cure for embarrassment, and your son knows nothing of it. You could yank your son's pants down in public and he'd just run around half-naked. Our kids sometimes yanked their *own* pants down to do just that, though not in public . . . wait. Does a family gathering count as public?

It might help to know everyone experiences this kind of thing. But, really, you just need to sever embarrassment from your mind. It does no good and it won't stop until your son goes to college, at which point he'll just be embarrassing himself.

I do not recommend joining in your son's activities to overcome embarrassment, however. A kid yelling "PENIS!" in a restaurant is very different from an adult doing it. Trust me. I know from experience.

*Parenthood*

# I FEEL LIKE I'M BEHIND THE CURVE

You made it through the newborn stage, the toddler stage, the "terrible twos," the "even more terrible threes," the "for the love of God fours," and "wait, it doesn't stop at preschool? fives." Now that your daughter goes to kindergarten, you high-five yourself and decide to make that celebratory margarita a Cadillac margarita because you somehow kept a human alive and well for half a decade.

But the celebration and the cocktail seem bittersweet because you don't feel any more ahead of the game than when you first welcomed her into the world. If anything, the fact that she now has a firm grasp of language means she can craft elaborate and vigorous arguments against anything you say, even things as simple as "Get dressed."

Once you start to understand how to handle one developmental stage, she enters another. The rules and the goals keep changing. It's like playing chess on a Monopoly board with pieces from Candyland ... in a tornado. The light at the end of the parenting tunnel must exist. At some point, it has to get easier, right? At some point, you actually just figure it out.

That's your hope, anyway, because the thought of constantly getting blindsided by parenting challenges frightens you beyond words. You've actually replaced that celebratory margarita with a full pint of vanilla swirl ice cream and you're now moving onto the block of aged cheddar in the fridge.

You've undoubtedly heard of the "It Gets Better" campaign, in which people share their stories of being gay in an effort to reassure LGBT youth that things can and do get better. They should make one for parents called "It Gets Different." And it should come with a flask or a subscription to some sort of Chocolate of the Week club. This feeling of always being one step behind won't go away because you always *will be* one step behind, probably two or three steps. You can't deal with something you've never experienced, and you don't experience it until it happens. So when your little girl hits a new developmental stage, you all get to go through it together. And though you may have gone through that stage yourself once, you haven't done it as a parent.

Of course: little kids, little problems; big kids, big problems. Hey, at least it's never boring, right? So enjoy the cocktail. Or the ice cream. Or the weeping. You'll need it.

*Parenthood*

# REAL PROBLEMS

# I DON'T KNOW WHAT ADVICE TO FOLLOW

When you watch an Aaron Sorkin show, you can keep up with nearly 80 percent of it. So you consider yourself an intelligent, well-informed member of society. If there's something about which you're curious, you do the research; you gather the information and make an educated decision on how to proceed. When you discovered you were soon to become a parent, however, you applied the same techniques and encountered a wall of disparate and impassioned rules for raising your child.

With a single click you went from a study showing the disastrous effects of the Cry-It-Out method of sleep training to an article espousing its many benefits. One YouTube video tells you why it's good to let your child help dictate his daily nap time, another explains how only a rigid schedule will prevent him from becoming a hoarder who spends his nights smearing himself with Nutella.

With so much varying information, you do the only thing you can—you apply all of it. You try a different technique each day, sometimes doubling up. You use the Cry-It-Out method for sleep training on Tuesday and spend the rest of the day employing Attachment Parenting. On Wednesday you try Tiger Mother Parenting by berating your newborn and then follow it with Helicopter Parenting while the grandparents visit. And for some reason, your Crying Tiger Attachment Helicopter method seems to have no effect on your baby.

 **CTFD**

The only thing you'll guarantee by applying techniques you don't need is that your child will have plenty of fodder for his tell-all memoir that makes *Mommie Dearest* look like *Mary Poppins.* You probably don't need a method (except for CTFD, obviously), you just need to parent. None of the experts agree, anyway; even the ones I consulted for this book disagreed on a few topics. So go with your instincts. Unless you're thinking of launching your baby from a trebuchet, your gut is usually right. If you do need some guidance, find the parenting technique that fits most with your personality. After all, you're the one who'll be using it every day. The baby just benefits from it. And just to be clear, Trebuchet Parenting is not a thing.

*Real Problems*

# I HAVEN'T STUDIED PARENTING AT ALL

When you announced your pregnancy, your family and friends sent you enough parenting books to open your own lending library. But unlike a library, these books all remain unread. Between prepping the baby's room, taking infant CPR classes, making sure things at work are covered so your maternity doesn't bring down the company and spark an economic collapse, you haven't had time to even take those tomes out of the boxes they came in, let alone actually read them. (Aside from that copy of *The Happiest Baby on the Block,* which you managed to skim just before using it to steady the wobbly china hutch.)

Then your delivery date comes and you're officially a parent, and you realize you'll have even less time now. And with the possible exception of *Full House* reruns, you've never bothered to watch any TV shows about parenting. You've done no practical research on parenthood, unless the three days spent debating which color to paint the accent wall in the nursery counts.

Your baby is in your home, in your *hands.* You both just stare blankly at each other, waiting for something to happen, waiting for a sign, some direction, some help.

## CTFD

You know how many parenting books you absolutely must read before or after having a baby? Exactly zero.

You have too much on your plate to worry about reading a dreary chapter on nap schedules. You'll find that your instincts work fine. But here are the basics:

- When the baby cries, attend to it.

- If you have any concerns, ask your pediatrician.

- Take time for yourself when you can.

- Don't throw the baby into a ceiling fan.

# I DON'T KNOW IF MY CHILD'S BEHAVIOR IS NORMAL

When your fourth college boyfriend in a year dumped you, you turned to your best friend. She'd been like a sister ever since junior high, when you'd both driven that snobby girl Tiffany from your circle of friends. Your best friend had a gift for making you feel better, but really you called her to hear if the same thing had ever happened to her. It eased your mind to know you weren't the only one experiencing such a romantic apocalypse.

So years later, when you realize your pregnancy has made your feet grow to a size rivaling the massive tootsies of a yeti, you ask your BFF during a playdate if she experienced the same thing. With a smirk, she reveals she replaced every pair of shoes she owned with exact replicas, two full sizes larger than before her pregnancy.

You sigh with relief and hoist your gargantuan dogs onto the ottoman as your child plays with her child. Then you notice her kid whine in anger and bring a Duplo block down on your son's head. You both leap to your very stable feet, but still can't prevent your boy from returning the blow with a wooden train. You apologize and your friend waves it off with a shrug, checking her kid for lasting damage. She seems so relaxed about such awful behavior.

A sour lovelife and huge feet are one thing, but this is quite another. With no control group in the room, you're left to just surmise that *both* of your children are terrible. At this moment, you regret ostracizing Tiffany. Having her here might offer some perspective. According to Facebook, her kids are incredibly well behaved.

## CTFD

It's natural to want to know if your child behaves like others, but don't go to such lengths to prove their normalcy that you stop strangers on the street to ask if their child can differentiate colors yet. Go ahead and check with your friends to ease your mind. Chances are, whatever irrational thing your child does, her kid does too. And if not, so what? Maybe her kid doesn't try to eat the purple glitter from the box of art supplies and yours thinks it's some sort of fairy pâté. That just means your child will have fabulously disco bowel movements.

## EVERYTHING COSTS TOO MUCH

Your daughter's legs hang over the front of the small stroller you got when she was born. She's growing and it's time to invest in a new one. You go online to research some options and have the same reaction to the prices that you did when you were first stocking your home for the baby's arrival: "These things must be made of some sort of rare metal or, perhaps, gemstones."

You're convinced parenting is some kind of scam. Bottles, breast pump, baby food, diapers, clothes, toys, and furniture—the list of necessities for your baby goes on longer than a fusion jazz quintet jam session. And they're all expensive. Plus, as your baby grows, you end up replacing items before they even lose their shine. Your current stroller doesn't even have a loose joint or scuffed wheel. With the exception of that time your girl spat up Cheerios and steamed carrots in it, the thing's like new.

A lot of parents look at a stroller choice as a reflection of their love for their child. The mother at the park with the tricked-out $1,700 Stokke Xplory stroller clearly loves her baby more than the mother with the $350 Baby Jogger City Mini GT. You need one that accurately demonstrates how much you love your daughter, even though, if it weren't for her, you'd have enough money to update your wardrobe a bit.

------------------ **CTFD** ------------------

For those of you expecting your first child, I didn't make up those names or prices. Happy shopping! But you should find friends or a group of moms who have kids slightly older than yours, because hand-me-downs cost exactly $0.

See, your baby doesn't care about what stroller you have or what brand of clothes you buy. For our twins, we bought two $15 umbrella strollers and one set of $13 stroller connectors. They're functional, they're super-light, they each fold up to the size of a poster tube, you can flip them open with one hand, and our guys don't know a Stokke stroller from a Bluetick Coonhound. And most of their clothes came from our friends. We saved enough money to purchase the Arizona Cardinals. We didn't actually *buy* the team, but we could've.

## THERE'S SOMETHING WRONG

You're a stage three yoga master, you have a cabinet full of green tea, and you're so relaxed that you fell asleep during your last root canal. Nothing shakes you. Nothing, that is, until you hear your pediatrician say some variation of the phrase, "There's something wrong."

You had a feeling your child had a medical (or psychological) issue, and as an observant parent, you kept a mental checklist of the signs. But, because you know to CTFD, you didn't panic. You remained levelheaded and sought the input of professionals. They ran tests and confirmed your fear. It is probably the only time in your life you hate that you were correct.

You don't want to flip out, but any such issue with your beloved child reduces you to a quivering wreck. How are you supposed to remain calm when your kid—the person you love most in the world, the creature that helped you become the person you are today—needs something you can't provide?

———————— **CTFD** ————————

It's OK. You can panic.

You're scared, you're angry, you're sad, and those feelings are completely justified. Allow yourself to feel them, go through all of them, wallow in them, and embrace them. Do this for an afternoon, and then get yourself together, because your child needs you.

All of the other instances in which you should CTFD help clear your mind for moments like this one. So barrel through it, then learn all you can from your pediatrician or psychologist about next steps. Look for support groups for people going through what you're about to go through, go to the meetings, contribute. Talk to people and share your story with trusted friends. Most importantly, however, let your child panic if he needs to. Because like you, he's scared, angry, and sad. You are his guide. He'll look to you to see how he's supposed to handle this.

So, yes, panic for a bit. But also be strong, have hope.

# I DISAGREE WITH MY DOCTOR

Your baby sneezes, and the unusual yellow tinge to the snot gets you wondering if it's more than a cold. So you go online, do a little research, and convince yourself the baby has a combination of the bubonic plague, leprosy, and gout.

When you call your pediatrician, however, she seems less than concerned. She doesn't even think you need to bring the child in for an exam and outright forbids you to follow through with your idea to give the baby a full-body Purell rubdown. But you see this nasal fluid and you know something biologically terrible brews inside your baby. I mean, you didn't even check to see if it could be a parasite.

Your three options are: bring the baby in for a doctor's visit anyway; start looking for a new pediatrician who shares your concern for golden mucus; go on the hunt for some black market antibiotics. You decide to start calling other doctors in town, since that's the path of least resistance. Many of them are more than eager to see you, as long as they take your insurance.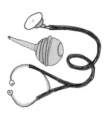

Thus begins your multi-stop tour of the local medical community. Along the way, you swing by the market for supplies, just in case you need to do that Purell rubdown after all.

## —————————— CTFD ——————————

Hopefully you interviewed at least a few pediatricians when you were expecting, and you landed on one you trust. If that's the case, don't start second-guessing the one person in the conversation who actually went to medical school. No pediatrician *wants* kids to get sick. Colds, stomach bugs, sore throats, diarrhea, ear infections, and more are all very common. When you describe what's going on in your initial call, your doctor can assess if you really need to come in or if it's just a matter of waiting it out. And even if you don't believe your chosen medical professional when she tells you your baby is fine, no doctor can refuse you the right to make an appointment. And if your intuition won't let up that your child needs medical care, get a second opinion. Just step away from the Purell.

## THE OTHER FOUR-LETTER WORD

Assuming you've read this book from front to back, you've now come to the end, where things get summarized and you're handed a nice little doggy bag of information you can take with you on your journey through parenthood. If you're one of those anarchistic types who reads the end first, congrats, you're spoiling the whole thing. Since you show a complete disregard for narrative structure, Rosebud is a sled. How do you like that?

Anyway, for the rest of you, hopefully you now understand that parenting need not incorporate an endless battle with stress. You've learned not to compare yourself or your child to other families, to pick your battles, and that it's really OK to feel like you don't have it figured out because you so totally don't. And if it helps, you probably never will. Really, just assume you're doing it wrong, so when things go right you'll be pleasantly surprised. That attitude got me through both my junior prom and my first job out of college.

Don't confuse all this talk of CTFD with "checking out." On the contrary, stay attentive, stay aware, and don't leave the oven on. And if the scenarios failed to resonate with you and if you will retain only one thing from this book, make it this last point:

### Love your child and the rest will follow.

You can have obsessive-compulsive disorder or a nervous tic or anger-management issues or an uncontrollable urge to purchase cowboy hats—whatever problems you think could keep you from parenting well, nothing matters more than loving your child. When the Beatles sang "All You Need Is Love," they didn't mean that's the only tool you need. They meant that tool helps you build other tools, structures, and devices. Love serves as the means by which you can build any type of parenting relationship, whether you want a shimmering museum displaying your greatness or a simple home to keep you all warm. So don't let stress or panic or worry or any of that stuff get in the way. And to clear the path for your love, just follow these two simple steps:

1. Calm the f*ck down.

2. There is no second step.

## ABOUT THE AUTHOR

David Vienna is a father of twin boys and the creator of the parenting Tumblr site TheDaddyComplex.com. Babble voted him one of the funniest dad bloggers in the world and The Daily Beast named his Twitter feed a "Beast Best." He's appeared on television and web shows to discuss parenting and social media. He was also an extra in the Robin Givens movie *Foreign Student*.